CW00540918

WORCESTERSHIRE
Family History
GUIDEBOOK

WORCESTERSHIRE
Family History
GUIDEBOOK

VANESSA MORGAN

The History Press

First published 2011

The History Press
The Mill, Brimscombe Port
Stroud, Gloucestershire, GL5 2QG
www.thehistorypress.co.uk

© Vanessa Morgan, 2011

The right of Vanessa Morgan to be identified as the Author
of this work has been asserted in accordance with the
Copyrights, Designs and Patents Act 1988.

All rights reserved. No part of this book may be reprinted
or reproduced or utilised in any form or by any electronic,
mechanical or other means, now known or hereafter invented,
including photocopying and recording, or in any information
storage or retrieval system, without the permission in writing
from the Publishers.

British Library Cataloguing in Publication Data.
A catalogue record for this book is available from the British Library.

ISBN 978 0 7524 5969 1

Typesetting and origination by The History Press
Printed in Great Britain
Manufacturing managed by Jellyfish Print Solutions Ltd

Contents

Introduction

Family history is one of the fastest growing hobbies in Britain and the second most popular topic on the Internet.

The beginnings of family history start with conversations with the rest of the family. What do they remember? Who do they remember? What stories were they told? And, most importantly, does anyone have any old certificates? Perhaps there are old photographs about. To put a face to a name is a fantastic opportunity.

But remember family legends may not always be completely accurate. Details passed from one generation to another can be a bit like Chinese whispers. An expression heard from grandma: 'I wonder if we're related to…?' Can, as the years progress, become: 'Well my mother always told me that her grandmother said we were related to…'

When you've collected as much of this information as you can, write it all down in an orderly way. Start using index cards for each individual you know about. Work out dates of birth from any death certificates you have; then you'll have some idea of where to start looking in the births or census for that particular person. The sooner you start getting into the habit of being organised the better. Once your family history really gets under way you'll be surprised how much paper work can be accumulated, even when you're using a computer!

Keep a notebook as a 'to-do' list so you're prepared for your next visit to the record office, or session on the Internet. There's nothing worse than coming home and finding you've totally forgotten to look for grandma's Aunt Bessie in the census.

You will probably find that you want to invest in a family history programme to store all your information electronically. There are many to choose from on the market today and they are always improving, so the best advice is to buy the latest genealogical magazine to see what they are reviewing that month. Or, if you get talking to another researcher in the record office, ask what they use. You will find fellow researchers are friendly and helpful; experienced researchers are always ready to give you advice. Joining a family history society is a great way to make new friends and get help.

An important thing you always have to remember with regards to family history is the spelling of names. This applies to all types of records and registers that you will come across while doing your research. You will also find place names and occupations that are spelt very differently from how they are today. As recently as the latter half of the nineteenth century the majority of the population couldn't even write, and those who could usually had their own ways of spelling. A name would be entered in a register in the way that the person with the pen thought it should be written, or how it had been pronounced. Sometimes people would learn how to write their name for official purposes, but they may not have learnt how to read, so do not be fooled if you see your ancestor has signed his name on his wedding day. An example I came across once in a marriage register was where the vicar had entered the groom's surname as Ainge but the groom had signed himself Haines! There are quite a number of Ainge births in the General Register Office indexes alone.

Another strange example that you may see is Alwens for Huins, or once again the dropped H off, making Arris instead of Harris. Sometimes an H may have been picked up as an M and the name Hilton becomes Milton, or vice versa. Other mistakes include the substitution of letters in the middle of a name, for example 'ie' for 'ea'. The first day I ever spent in a record office I missed my great-grandfather's baptism because I had always known

Ask around the family for any old photographs. Pictures like these can make an attractive addition to the family tree. These show a wedding from 1920; a family group c.1905; and a typical early 1920s family (*Overleaf*).

the spelling of his name as Pearce – but here it had been written as Pierce, and in my ignorance I dismissed it. Try making a list of each surname and how many ways you think that name could be spelt. This could also be a good party game – the winner is the name with the most variations.

Christian names, too, can be deceiving. Perhaps you or your family knew of an Uncle Harry. You may assume he was Harold. But I remember a great uncle by the name of Harry and when I started my research I found his name was John Henry. From how many christian names does the name Bert derive – Albert, Bertram, Gilbert, Herbert, Hubert, Robert or Wilbert. And was he Bert or Bertie? If using an index on an Internet site which uses a wildcard (i.e. ★) add the ★ at the end of Bert, then if he was Bertie he will be found. Most Internet sites have a wildcard tool and these are extremely useful in finding odd spellings of surnames too.

Ages can also fool you, probably due to that fact that many people perhaps did not celebrate birthdays, and the older they got the more they lost track of their age. You may find that an age on a death certificate doesn't agree with what you already know about your ancestor. Look at who registered the death and ask yourself: would that person really know how old the deceased was? Did they just give an approximate figure? When searching for a birth or baptism, or someone in a census index, always allow up to five years either side of a given date; you can never be sure. William Avery, talking about his birth in his memoirs *Old Redditch* in the 1800s, wrote:

Though present at the event I cannot fix the date, but I may say I came in with the nineteenth century. I was anxious to have noted down the exact date, but on looking over the register I found that when it was removed from the Old Abbey Chapel to the New Chapel on the Green waste paper was a scarce commodity, and many leaves, including that one which my name was inscribed, had been utilised to wrap up 'dabs' of hooks sent into the factory.

So William went through his life not really knowing how old he was.

Family history can be a very frustrating hobby, so remember: the more branches you research the more you can build on your tree. Research can come to a halt where two baptisms are found in an ancestor's name and you don't know which is your relative's. By following other branches until you can (hopefully) find an answer, you can move to another line; because you have two grandfathers and two grandmothers, you already have four branches to follow. The next generation immediately doubles the number of branches. Unfortunately, there are one or two pitfalls you will come across during your research, but the more experienced you become the more you can learn to accept these problems and go on to other parts of your tree.

Of course, if some of your ancestors stayed in one parish this is a real bonus as you can follow them back through the registers with great ease. But don't be fooled into thinking people did not move around, because they did, and it can be surprising how far a family, or individual, was willing to go to find better working conditions or a better life. I'm not just talking about emigrating to another country; people moved quite regularly around England, particularly during the 1800s when the Industrial Revolution was at its height. A look at the 1851 census for Worcestershire will show how people living in the industrial areas had moved in from the countryside. But the thrill of finding someone by accident is what family history is all about.

So a good general rule is to remember people in past times were not so precise or particular when giving their details, or any information about themselves, as we are now. Even educated people were not always that particular with their spelling. In his diary the Reverend William Lea of St Peter's, Droitwich, who was educated at Rugby School and Brasenose College, Oxford, spelt a local teacher's name as Mr Jeycock in 1863. But nineteen years later in 1882, he spelt it as Jeacock.

The County of Worcestershire

The area that was to become known as Worcestershire was settled by the Romans from about AD 50 onwards. They had arrived to find not just a boggy forest, but a river that had great potential. So they began to develop the region. Soon three Roman roads met here: Watling Street (London to Chester); Akeman Street (Newbury to Gloucester); and the Fosse Way (Exeter to Lincoln). Small towns were built, the principle of these being Roman Sainae, better known today as Droitwich.

Roman rule came to an end in the fifth century and Worcester was left to decline until the seventh century, when the Saxons arrived. Now the town began to form on a ford by the banks of the River Severn. There are conflicting theories on the origins of Worcester's name; one traces it to the Saxon word 'Wire-cester' meaning a 'place of wears'. Another holds that the Saxons used a derivative of 'Ceaster', the Roman name for settlement, and added the word 'wogoran' meaning 'people of the winding river'. In AD 680 Worcester became the seat of a bishop and with this the town began to grow in importance. The church was a very powerful body then, so having a bishop in residence gave a town an important position over its neighbours. Domesday Book states that Worcester had a population of 2,000 and that by the start of the thirteenth century it was surrounded by a city wall.

When one thinks of the history of Worcester perhaps the first thing that comes to mind is the Battle of Worcester in 1651, when Oliver Cromwell

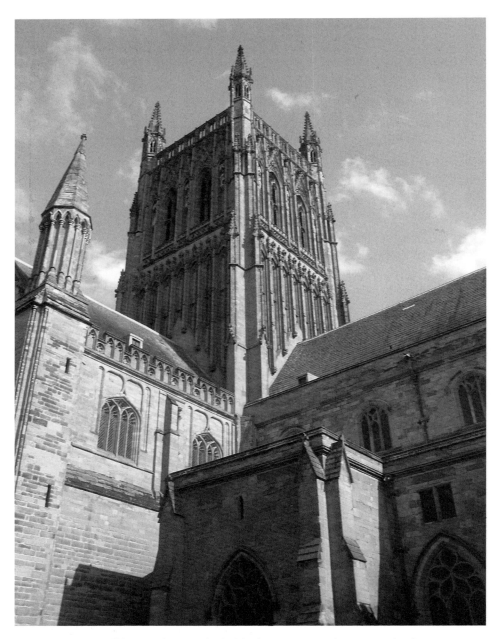

Worcester is well known for its cathedral, built in 1084. On the opposite bank is the county cricket ground and the view of the cathedral makes it one of the most attractive grounds in England.

defeated King Charles II. However, it was also Worcester that featured in the first battle of the Civil War, at nearby Powick Bridge on 22 September 1642. Worcester was very much a Royalist stronghold and suffered considerable damage throughout the war. It was some time before renovations took place, but by the 1700s reconstruction had begun. This is evident in the number of Georgian buildings in Worcester, particularly in the Foregate, Tything and Barbourne areas. The present bridge across the Severn was built in 1781, replacing the old medieval one.

When the Pilgrim Fathers stepped from the *Mayflower* in 1620, one of the members of that first group of colonists was Edward Winslow, from a Worcestershire family. He had been baptised at St Peter's, Droitwich, on 20 October 1595. A note later written in the parish register, on the inside front cover states:

> In this register is recorded the baptism of Edward Winslow, a pilgrim father, on 20 October 1595.

Edward's brother Gilbert, who also travelled on the *Mayflower*, had been baptised on 29 October 1600. Their parents, Edward and Magdalen, had married on 3 November 1594 – a scribbled note states the marriage had taken place in London.

Worcestershire also had the notoriety of being associated with the Gunpowder Plot. Brothers Robert and Thomas Wintour (or Winter) lived at Huddington Court in Huddington, about 4 miles east of Worcester, and they belonged to the principal group of the thirteen plotters. Thomas was one of the first to be approached by Robert Catesby, and it was he who recruited Guy Fawkes. Robert Winter may have helped dig an abortive tunnel under the Palace of Westminster and their younger brother, John, was also convicted and executed for being involved in a minor role.

There are many other famous Worcestershire people, some better known than others. Edward Elgar was born in Broadheath on 22 June 1857. He was the son of an organist and music dealer, and at the time of the 1861 census, the family were living at College Yard in the St Michael's parish of Worcester. On leaving school in 1872, Edward started working as a clerk for a solicitor but stayed for just four months. By 1881 he was a professor of the violin and lodging with Martha Grafton in Claines. He had had some lessons on the violin in London but was basically self-taught.

Biographers say that Elgar succeeded his father William as organist at St George's Roman Catholic Church, Worcester, in 1885 – but according to the 1891 census he is living in Fulham, London, with his wife Caroline. It was at St George's that he started writing music and by 1901, when he was living at Craiglea, Main Road, Malvern Wells he was a 'composer of music'.

Hannah Snell was born in Worcester in 1723. She was the daughter of Samuel Snell, a hosier and dyer, and his wife Mary. When she was twenty she met a Dutch seaman, James Summs, and married him, but he deserted her soon after she found she was pregnant. Her daughter died and the lovesick young wife was determined to find her husband. She borrowed some clothes from her brother-in-law, James Gray, and, using his name, went in search of her husband. The story goes that she was press-ganged into joining a regiment of foot and, after marching to Carlisle, spent some time serving during the Jacobite Rebellion of 1745. But this has never been proven.

What is certain, however, is that in the 1740s Snell joined the Royal Marines at Portsmouth and sailed to the East Indies. Despite being wounded she still managed to conceal her true identity, and over a period of two years she served on two ships. Whilst in Lisbon she discovered her husband had been executed, and on returning to Gravesend in 1750, she admitted the deception. Her career moved to the stage and, dressed as a soldier, she entertained her audience by singing ballads. She successfully petitioned to become a Chelsea Pensioner and due to her wounds received a pension. Marrying a second time she had two children but started to develop symptoms of insanity. She ended her days in Bedlam (also known as Bethlehem) Hospital and died in 1792. Her body is buried at Chelsea Hospital.

Alfred Edward Housman, the poet best known for his book of verse *A Shropshire Lad*, was born in Bromsgrove in 1859. He studied at The Bromsgrove School (where he later taught for a short time). In 1861, 1871 and 1881 the family was living at Kidderminster Road, Bromsgrove. His father Edward was a solicitor. In 1881 Alfred was an undergraduate at St

John's College, Oxford. He was a clerk in the patent office in 1891 and lodging with Elizabeth Taylor in Hornsey, Middlesex. Still in Hornsey in 1901 he had become a 'professor at university'.

Alfred's brother Lawrence was born in 1865 and also became a writer and playwright. His play *Victoria Regina* was produced on Broadway in 1935. Due to a parliamentary law stating that stage productions depicting Queen Victoria could not be produced until 100 years after her succession, the play did not reach London until 1937 when it was produced at the Lyric Theatre. It was made into a film in 1938. Lawrence, too, moved from Worcestershire and was living in Kensington in 1891, working as a designer and draughtsman. In 1901 he was in Battersea and gave his occupation as an author and artist.

Stanley Baldwin was born in Bewdley in 1867 and was educated at Harrow and Cambridge. He was the son of Alfred Baldwin, an industrialist from Stourport. Baldwin's Ltd was an iron foundry and the 1871 census shows that Alfred employed 400 people. The family lived at Wilton House, Hartlebury. In 1881 Stanley was a scholar at St Michael's School in Langley, Buckinghamshire. In 1891 he was staying with his uncle, Edward Bourne-Jones, an iron master, at 49 North End Road, Fulham. In 1901 the whole family was in Bournemouth. In 1908 Stanley Baldwin became the Conservative MP for Bewdley, rising to the position of Chancellor of the Exchequer in 1922, and then Prime Minister in 1923.

Rowland Hill was born in Kidderminster in 1795 and was the son of a schoolmaster. He invented the postage stamp, revolutionising the postal system. In 1837 he had written a booklet about how the post office could be reformed. The postal service then was very expensive; different amounts were charged depending on the number of pages and the distance to be sent. Hill suggested that people should pay only according to the weight of the letter. In 1839 the government asked him to look into his idea, and in 1840 the Penny Black was introduced. Although born in Kidderminster he only spent a short period of his life there. The 1851 census shows him living in Hamstead with his wife Caroline. His occupation was 'secretary to Post Master General'. In the 1871 census he was referred to as Sir Rowland Hill. He died in 1879.

Although associated with Oxford, William Morris was born in Hallow, Worcester, in 1877. The family moved to Oxford when he was aged three. He started working for a bicycle repairer and seller when he was aged fifteen then opened his own shop. He went on to work on motorcycles and then on cars. The Morris Oxford was produced in 1913 and the Morris Minor in 1928.

The Worcestershire Hundreds

A hundred is the old term used to describe the different administrative areas of the county. Set up in the tenth century, these courts had the power to deal with cases within their own hundred including tax, military and judicial matters. By the seventeenth century the power of the hundred had practically disappeared, and by the latter half of the 1800s these courts had ceased to operate. But for certain records and maps it may be necessary to know into which hundred the parish you are researching fell. Worcestershire is split into five hundreds: Blackenhurst Hundreds, Doddingtree Hundreds, Halfshire Hundreds, Oswaldslow Hundreds and the Pershore Hundreds:

Blackenhurst, South East Worcestershire. The upper division includes Aldington, Badsey, Bretforton, Church Honeybourne, The Littletons, Offenham and Wickhamford. The lower division Abbots Morton, Atch Lench, Bengeworth, Evesham, Hampton (Great & Little), Norton Lenchwick, Oldberrow and Sheriffs Lench.

Doddingtree, West Worcestershire. The upper division includes Acton Beauchamp, Alfrick, Areley-Kings, Berrington, Bockleton, Clifton-on-Teme, Cotheridge, Eastham, Edwin-Loach, Hanley-Child, Hanley-William, Hilhampton, Kyre-Minor, Kyre-Wyard, Lulsley, Martley, Orleton, Sapey-Pritchard, Shelsley-Kings, Shelsley-Walsh, Stanford, Suckley, Sutton and Tenbury. The lower division Abberley, Alton, Astley, Bayton, Bewdley, Doddenham, Mamble, Ribbesford, Shelsley-Beauchamp, Shrawley and Stockton.

Halfshire, in North East Worcestershire. The upper division includes Bromsgrove, Church-Lench, Cofton-Hacket, part of Crowle,

Dodderhill, Doverdale, Droitwich, Elmbridge, Feckenham, Grafton-Manor and Hadsor.

Oswaldslow, Central & South Worcestershire. The upper division includes Alderminster, Armscott, Blackwell, Blockley, Cleeve Prior, Cutsdean, Dailsford, Darlingscot, Ditchford, Dorne, Draycot, Evenload, Iccomb, Newbold, Shipston-upon-Stour, Tidmington and Tredington. The middle division, Alston, Alvechurch, Bishampton, Bredon and Norton, Charlton, Conderton, Cropthorne, Crowle (part), Elmley Castle, Fladbury, Hanbury, Harvington, Hill and Moor, Himbleton, Huddington, Inkberrow, The Lenches, Overbury, Sedgeberrow, Stock and Bradley, Stoke Prior, Teddington, Tibberton, Throckmorton, Washbourne and Wyre Piddle. The lower division Berrow, Bredicot, Broadwas, Churchill, Claines, Crome d'Abitot, Earls Crome, Grimley, Hallow, Hartlebury, Hill-Crome, Hindlip, Holt, St John's Bedwardine, Kempsey and Norton, Knightwick, Knighton, Lindridge, Little Malvern, Oddingley, Ombersley, Pendock, Pensax, Redmarley d'Abitot, Ripple, Spetchley, Stoulton, Tything of Whiston, Warndon, Welland, Whittington, White Ladies Aston, Wichenford, Wick (Part) and Wolverley.

Pershore, Central & South Worcestershire. The upper division includes Abberton, Beoley, Besford, Birlingham, Bricklehampton, Broadway, Broughton Hacket, Comberton (Great & Little), Defford, Dormston, Eckington, Flyford Flavel, Grafton Flyford, Martin Hussingtree, Naunton Beauchamp, North Piddle, Pershore, Pinvin, Pirton, Pensham, Peopleton, Strensham, Upton Snodsbury, Wick (part), Walcot and Yardley. The lower division Bransford, Birtsmorton, Bushley, Castle Morton, Chaseley, Eldersfield, Great Malvern, Hanley Castle, Leigh, Longdon, Madresfield, Mathon, Newland, Powick, Queenhill, Severn Stoke, Staunton and Upton on Severn.

The county boundaries were unique in that there were a number of islands in other counties. These were Alstone, Daylesford and Little Washbourne; the registers for these parishes are still held in Worcester Family History Centre. Transcripts are held for Blockley, Tredington and Tidmington. Whereas there are no records for Alderminster, Cutsdean,

Edvin Loach, Evenlode, Iccomb and Shipston. In 1930 the county border changes meant that these disappeared and were lost to other counties. The parishes of Alderminster, Shipston, Tidmington and Tredington were moved to Warwickshire. Blockley, Chaceley, Cutsdean, Dayleford, Evenlode, Redmarley d'Abitot, Staunton and Teddington were moved to Gloucestershire.

Worcestershire's Landscape

The landscape of Worcestershire is one of contrasts. There are the hills: the Lickeys, Clent and the Malverns. The Malverns, a 9-mile chain rising from the vast flatness of the Severn Plain, provide a natural border between Worcestershire and Herefordshire. The Lickeys and Clent run across the north-east of the county. Bredon Hill, epitomised in the poem *A Shropshire Lad* by A.E. Houseman, overlooks the Vale of Evesham and the River Avon.

The Severn runs through the county from the north to south, through Bewdley, Stourport (where it is joined by the Stour), the villages of Shrawley, Grimley and Holt, and then on to Worcester. From there it winds its way through Severn Stoke and Upton on Severn to Tewkesbury in Gloucestershire. Before joining the Severn, the Stour has run through Stourbrige, Wolverley and Kidderminster. The Teme flows from Tenbury through to Powick where it joins the Severn just below Worcester, acting as a natural border between Shropshire and Worcestershire. And the Avon travels through the south-east of the county at Evesham and Pershore where it then meets the Severn at Tewkesbury.

Post Office directories in the 1800s described Worcestershire as being very uneven in shape; its length from north to south is about 34 miles, and its width about 30 miles. It was described as being one of the 'finest' counties in England with plenty of woodlands, hills and pastureland. The ground was of a good quality; in many parts it was very rich and fertile, which had made it an excellent area for farming and market gardening. Wheat, barley, beans, hops and fruit were grown in abundance. Whilst in the rivers could be found salmon, trout, grayling, shad and lampreys.

Although there were patches of strong clay soil in certain parts, these were lighter in the east. Between Worcester and the Vale of Evesham the soil was deep and rich, in part alluvial. On the borders around the Cotswold Hills there was more limestone, with the lower regions being of a rich loam. From Worcester to the Malvern Hills the ground was more clay and gravel. And around the north of Stourbridge there was a large quantity of fire clay, so there were numerous firebrick furnaces in operation there. Stourbridge clay was also considered to be one of the best for making glass. A dark blue clay in Amblecote was very popular in the late seventeenth century for this reason.

A trade directory of 1876 described the geology of Worcestershire. The coal beds in the north-east were huge and there was a possibility of future extensions to the mines. The Bewdley coal basin in the north-west of Worcestershire was worked at Mamble, Rock and Bayton. The Forest of Wyre coal field was a broad strip stretching from the Abberley Hills and Bewdley and Billingsley. However, when it reached the right bank of the Severn it was only about a mile wide, less in certain sections. The Dudley coal basin was in the north, which also contained beds of iron ore.

Brine springs could be found in Droitwich and the neighbouring Stoke Prior. The brine was found in what was described as a 'sort of subterranean reservoir'. The floor was made of rock salt and the roof of gypsum. When the roof was pierced with boring equipment the brine shot to the surface like a fountain.

The coal mines employed 2,000 people and 8,000 were employed in the manufacture of hardware. In this group 6,000 were employed as nailers. The rest in the manufacture of such commodities as needles, fish hooks, tools, fenders, fire irons, shovels, scuttles, pans, hinges, screws, rivets, swords, cutlery and steel toys. The iron manufacturers employed 1,200, mainly in the north of the county. The glass works at Dudley and Stourbridge employed 400 people, the porcelain works in Worcester 500; 400 worked in brick making.

There was glove making and coach building in Worcester and carpet and rug manufacturing in Kidderminster. Others were employed at numerous other trades around the county which included salt, alkali, vinegar and vitriol working, brewing, malting, coke burning, tanning, comb, crate, lantern and button making, leather staining and paper manufacturing.

The *The Victoria County History* of Worcestershire volumes state that Worcestershire did have a monopoly in one industry – needle making. The trade began in Buckinghamshire where a Christopher Greening founded the industry in Long Crendon in the mid-sixteenth century. But when the needle making trade grew in importance in Redditch in the early nineteenth century, the Buckinghamshire workers moved there to find the work they were loosing in their own town. From then the industry grew and grew.

Up to the 1840s, before the arrival of the railways, the Severn could be described as the busiest commercial river in the country. Upstream the industrial revolution had its foundations in the Black Country. Downstream was the Bristol Channel, and from there, the rest of the world. Every riverside town, village or hamlet had a quay where sailing vessels travelling from Bristol to Worcester could rest. It was the Severn that had brought the Romans into the very heart of the country, followed by the Saxons and the Danes. The Normans carried their Caen stone up the Severn to build Worcester Cathedral, and from as early as the 1500s coal and iron had been taken up and down the river. In the eighteenth century the highest number of river coal tax collectors in the country were stationed in Worcester. Pottery from Broseley and Coalport in Shropshire was also brought down the river to be decorated at Worcester. At its height the Severn at Worcester could be crammed with over 100 boats. An 1884 directory stated that the river could hold ships of 80 tons at Worcester and 60 tons at Bewdley.

The earliest vessel on the Severn was a coracle. A small keelless boat, with its frame made of basket and sometimes covered in animal skins, it was mainly used for crossing the river. The first barge was a flat-bottomed, steep-sided trow. Some were small with a single square sail and more suited to the shallow waters of the upper parts of the Severn. Whereas the larger multi-sail trows could be used for travelling right down river into the more hazardous waters of the Bristol Channel. The main feature of these flat-bottomed boats was their ability to rest on mud flats and banks any where along the river, allowing cargo to be dropped at villages without the facility of a quay.

But with the arrival of the railways the use of the river in industry declined. Now it found itself a new industry – the pleasure boat. Today it has quite a thriving holiday trade, with both pleasure cruisers and long boats plying the river between Stourport and Gloucestershire. Upstream from Stourport the river is more suitable for canoes and rowing boats. There is also a network of numerous canals running through the county, so you may find ancestors who were connected to the waterways in some way. 'Waterman' is a term that covers most occupations connected to the rivers or canals, while a 'boatman' worked specifically on the boats, travelling the waterways.

The Staffordshire Worcester Canal opened in 1772. It ends its journey at Stourport where it meets the Severn after a 46-mile journey from the Trent and Mersey canal junction at Great Haywood. Intended for the easier transportation of coal, steel and carpets, it was designed as part of a section of the 'Grand Cross'; a system of canals designed by James Brindley to link the Mersey, the Trent, the Severn and the Thames.

Stourport, the thriving waterway town once known as the small parish of Lower Mitton, developed quickly when the canal was built. Shown here is one of the four remaining basins of the original five, now developed for holidaymakers. The old warehouses, now modernised, are still prominent.

The Worcester and Birmingham Canal starts at the River Severn in the Diglis Basin and travels for 16 miles through fifty-six locks, including the well-known Tardebigge Flight of thirty locks, before reaching the Birmingham plateau. It enters the grounds of Birmingham University, where at Selly Oak it once joined the Dudley No. 2 canal (there is no longer a link here now). On reaching the Gas Street Basin it then joins the Birmingham Canal. It is also connected to the Stratford Canal at Kings Norton. During this journey it also negotiated five tunnels, including the Kings Norton tunnel, which is nearly 2 miles long.

The Act authorising the construction of the canal was passed in 1791 but it was not opened until 1815. The engineering and construction had met with difficulties which had not been considered. It was constructed to carry the rapidly increasing quantities of raw materials and goods being produced in Birmingham and the Black Country, and to shave 30 miles off the old route down the river through Stourport. Trade was mainly

The Worcester and Birmingham Canal passing through Stoke Prior. In its heyday barges would travel up and down, heavily laden with salt, coal and other merchandise, between the Black Country and Worcester.

coal, salt, limestone, building materials, wood, chemicals and general merchandise. However for a short time there was a passenger service between Alvechurch and Birmingham. But not all day-visitors who travelled the canal from Birmingham were always welcome, as this report from the *Bromsgrove, Droitwich and Redditch Weekly Messenger* for Saturday 16 August 1873 shows:

On Monday, a boat load of the roughest of the rough patronised the pleasant neighbourhood of Hopwood, near Alvechurch, as a gypsy party, arriving about noon. They chose, among other amusements, to enter the garden of a person named Russell, amusing themselves by destroying all before them. They then commenced stripping the apple tress, and on being remonstrated with by a boatman and his wife, who were in charge of a load of coals (the property of Mr Reachall, who had a wharf at Alvechurch), they turned upon their remonstrates, savagely assaulted them, so that their clothing was saturated in blood. It was probably not within their knowledge that Mr Reachall also occupies a wharf at Kings Norton, which, on their return they must pass. The news having reached this place of the savage attack upon the boatman and his wife, their fellow work people determined to administer lynch law; having provided themselves with cuttings from trees – which could scarcely be denominated switches – they awaited the return of the roughs in the cool of the evening, and, it appears, administered such a castigation as will probably cause the party to consider before they repeat their brutal conduct in these parts.

Although 'lynching' is often a term used to describe a hanging by an angry crowd, the lynch law also referred to groups who took matters into their hands; to inflict punishment for a crime in other ways short of actual murder.

The last commercial barges on the Worcester and Birmingham canal made their final journeys in the 1960s. They had continued to be used by Cadbury's to carry chocolate from Bourneville, and coal companies to deliver coal to the Royal Porcelain factory.

In 1767 James Brindley was asked by Droitwich officials to survey access from the River Severn to the salt pits. In 1771 a short canal was opened to carry barges known as wich boats, a version of the old Severn trow, to the River Severn at Claines. The Droitwich Junction Canal opened in 1854 as a link from the old 'barge' canal to the Worcester and Birmingham Canal at Hanbury. This was one of the last canals to be built in England. It was also too late, as much of the salt traffic had already been transferred to the new Birmingham and Gloucester Railway Company. Further loss was felt when the Oxford, Worcester and Wolverhampton Railway was opened.

The building of the Dudley Tunnel Canal started in 1775 as an extension from the Birmingham canal in Tipton to the collieries and limestone mines at Castle Hill. It was completed in 1778 with another section, the Stourbridge Canal, opening in 1779. This brought supplies of coal to the glass industry of Stourbridge. The Dudley No. 1 was completed in 1792 and continued the link into Dudley at the Delph Locks. Here is the well-known tunnel which stretches under the town for 3,000 yards. It was hard work to negotiate as it had to be 'legged through' and was very claustrophobic. Dudley No. 2 canal was opened in 1798 and ran from Dudley to the Birmingham Worcester canal at Selly Oak. However only the 10 miles to Hawne Basin in Halesowen exist today.

The 1850s and 1860s were a busy time in Worcestershire with the building of many railway lines. This gave work to many people, not only with the laying of the tracks, but the building of the stations too. Worcester Shrub Hill station was built in 1850, opening on 5 October, and Foregate Street Station in 1860, opening on 17 May. The first major station on the Oxford, Wolverhampton and Worcester line was in Dudley and opened on 20 December 1852. The main lines, their branches and stations were opened in stages.

The Birmingham and Gloucester line which ran through Worcestershire via Kings Norton, Bromsgrove, Droitwich, Spetchley, Worcester, Defford, Eckington and Bredon, was among one of the earliest lines to be built. It was built as a link between the factories of Birmingham and the docks at Bristol, a journey which, by canal, took almost a week. For ten years from 1824 numerous surveys were undertaken; all saw a problem where the track would have to negotiate the steep Lickey incline. Eventually, in 1836, an agreement was made and work on the line began almost immediately.

The first section of the line, from Cheltenham to Bromsgrove, was finished by 1840, with a coach link to Birmingham. The line to Birmingham was completed a year later when it reached Camp Hill and joined the Birmingham to London line.

The people of Bromsgrove had not been happy at first to have a line run through their town, but an agreement was reached whereby the station would actually be built 2 miles out of the town at Aston Fields. Nevertheless, the railway gave the nail makers of Bromsgrove another choice of employment.

The Bromsgrove to Birmingham line passed through Barnt Green and it was here that a branch line went out through Alvechurch and Redditch in 1859. By 1868 the line had continued to Evesham and Ashchurch. A line was laid from Worcester to Norton and Abbottswood in 1850, then Norton to Evesham in 1852, and Evesham to Wolvercote (Oxford) in 1853. In February 1852 the line from Worcester to Droitwich opened with a spur to the Stoke Works to carry the salt. A few months later, in May, the line continued to Stourbridge, then on to Dudley in December.

The Worcester to Malvern and Hereford line opened in stages between 1859 and 1861. Malvern to Henwick in 1859, Henwick to Worcester Shrub Hill in 1860 and Malvern to Hereford in 1861. The Severn Valley railway was completed between Hartlebury and Shrewsbury in 1862 and a loop to pass through Kidderminster and Bewdley was completed in 1878.

According to a Worcestershire directory of 1884 there were two railway systems operating in the county – The Great Western and The Midland. The Great Western travelled via Church Honeybourne, Evesham, Pershore, Worcester, Droitwich, Hartlebury, Stourbridge, Dudley and then on to Wolverhampton. There were various branch lines which included the Worcester and Hereford line which eventually went out to Wales. A line also went from Stourbridge through Cradley to Rowley Regis and Birmingham. And the Severn Valley line from Hartlebury called at Stourport and Bewdley on its way to Shrewsbury. The branch line from Bewdley went out to Tenbury, and also to Kidderminster.

The Midland Railway – which was the Birmingham to Bristol line – called at Kings Norton, Bromsgrove, Droitwich and Worcester. It had a branch line at Kings Norton out to Halesowen and the branch line at Barnt Green to Redditch, Alcester and Evesham. Whilst a branch line on the Ashchurch to Tewkesbury section in Gloucestershire took in Upton on Severn and Great Malvern.

Registration Districts of Worcestershire

In 1836 two Acts of Parliament were passed – the Births and Deaths Registration Act and the Marriage Registration Act – which meant that from July 1837 all births, marriages and deaths were to be recorded. Each year was split into quarters – March, June, September and December – each covering the events of the previous three months. A General Register Office (GRO) was established and a registrar general appointed. He in turn appointed registrars and superintendent registrars for the rest of the country.

Like all other parts of England and Wales, Worcestershire was split into different registration districts, and each district had its own register office. There are maps in Worcester Family History Centre which illustrate where the different districts of Worcester are.

Over the years there were three changes in district boundaries and these maps also cover those changes: 1837–51, 1852–1946 and 1947–65. However, they only show the volume number and reference, and the larger register offices. If you are good at guesswork you may be able to read the map in relation to your family's parish, and decide in which district your family's events would have been registered. Alternatively, when an entry is found in the GRO indexes, look at a modern map to see how close this particular district is to the parish your ancestor lived. However, a good source of confirming which parishes belong to certain registration districts can also be found at www.ukbmd.org.uk. As with all research, unless a digitalised original image is displayed, it always has to be assumed there may be human error in the transcription, but this particular site does seem to be very accurate.

Some of the boundaries overlap into other counties so you may find an event registered in a different county. For example, anything taking place in the parishes of Feckenham, Inkberrow and their smaller neighbours was registered in Alcester – although in later years these parishes were moved to Bromsgrove.

In recent years registers have been passed to a central office. Most of the registers for Worcestershire are now held in the register office at County Hall, Worcester. However, one or two are now held outside the county; some districts in the north of the county have been divided between Birmingham, Sandwell (West Bromwich) and Dudley. So if your ancestor was born in, say, Kings Norton, you will have to apply to Birmingham Register Office for the certificate. Certain parishes in the south of the county have been transferred to the North Cotswold district.

When purchasing a certificate the best course of action, if you know you have found the correct entry, is to apply to the GRO giving the year, quarter

An original full birth certificate. A document which you may find at the back of a drawer. You would now be in a position to search for the marriage of a James Henry Hill and Hilda Pearce. Indeed it can be found in the Alcester District during the December quarter 1911.

BIRTHS AND DEATHS REGISTRATION ACT, 1874.

CERTIFICATE of REGISTRY of BIRTH.

I, the undersigned, Do hereby certify that the Birth of

Hilda Pearce

born on the 19th day of January 1889 has been duly registered by me.

Witness my hand, this 25th day of February 1889

Joseph Johnson Registrar of Births and Deaths.

Feckenham Sub-District.

[OVER.]

When registering a birth, parents could pay a smaller fee and have a short birth certificate such as this. Not as helpful for a family historian, but as long as you have the date of birth you can find the entry in the GRO births index in order to obtain a copy of the full birth certificate. From there you can further your research..

Certified Copy of an Entry of Marriage.

Pursuant to The Births, Deaths, and Marriage Registration Acts, 1836 to 1898.

Superintendent Registrar's District of ALCESTER.

Marriage Solemnized at The Baptist Chapel Alcester in the District of ALCESTER, in the Counties of WARWICK AND WORCESTER.

When Married.	Name and Surname.	Age.	Condition.	Rank or Profession.	Residence at the time of Marriage.	Father's Name and Surname.	Rank or Profession
Eleventh November 1911	James Henry Hill	21 years	Bachelor	Machinist at a Cycle Factory	42 Mount Pleasant Redditch	David Hill	Cycle builder
	Hilda Pearce	22 years	Spinster	Needle Finisher	Bark Lane Astwood Bank	John Thomas Pearce	Needle straightener

in the Baptist Chapel, according to the Rites and Ceremonies of the Baptists, by certificate

Marriage solemnized between us, J. H. Hill / H Pearce in the Presence of us, John Thomas Pearce / Lily Duffin — J. H. Andrews Min / A H Whitehead Reg

ALFRED HENRY WHITEHEAD, Registrar of Marriages for the District of ALCESTER, in the Counties of WARWICK AND WORCESTER Certify that this is a True Copy of the Entry No. 6 in the Register Book of Marriages for the said District and that such Register is in my custody. Witness my hand this 30th day of October 1915

Statutory Fees payable for an ordinary Certified Copy of an entry in a Register of Births, Deaths, or Marriages, if taken at the time of registration, are 2s. 7d. 1d. for the stamp), but if taken at any time afterwards, an additional fee of 1/- in chargeable for a search extending over a period of not more than one year; additional for every additional year.

This marriage certificate is not the original as it is dated 30 October 1915. Perhaps the original was lost and a copy needed to be obtained. Perhaps James was going to enlist and needed to show his marriage certificate. It shows the place, the names, occupations and fathers' names. Often the exact age isn't given. Full age means they were over the age of 21. A minor would be under the age of 21.

and reference (volume and page number). This can be done online at www.gro.gov.uk/gro. But how do you know you have the right entry? In marriages it is very easy if you know the surnames of both the parties. The GRO reference number (i.e. volume and page number) and the registration district will be identical under the two names in the GRO index. For example, the marriage of John Duffin and Ann Ingram in Alvechurch on 13 October 1850 will be found in the December quarter in the Bromsgrove district. Looking under the Ds for John's name in the GRO indexes we find a volume number of XVIII and page number 341. Looking for Ann Ingram in the same quarter, you will find the district of Bromsgrove and the reference, volume XVIII page 341, is the same. From the March quarter 1912 the spouse's name was included on the index, which simplifies the search.

From July 1911 births in the GRO index included the mother's maiden name. So if you know this, and you have the right district, you can be certain you have the right birth. This can also be particularly useful in locating siblings; looking for births of one surname in the same district with the same mother's maiden name. In some cases, particularly prior to 1911, you may be unsure whether you have the correct birth. For example, if it is a common name and a largely populated district, you are very likely to find more than one child with the same name. In cases like this it is best to contact the register office in question with the possible entries you have found, giving as many details as possible, especially the father's name. The registrar will check these and send the correct certificate. If none is correct they will return your cheque. However, they generally won't give a reason, or details of the various entries, only that the details do not agree with the information you have provided.

Indexes for the GRO indexes are kept at Worcester Family History Centre but can also be accessed online. The two popular sites are www.ancestry.co.uk and www.findmypast.co.uk. Both are subscription sites but they do enable you to do your research from the comfort of your own home. Worcester Family History Centre and many libraries do offer free online access to the library edition of Ancestry. Ancestry offers a quick name search, but as with all indexes the golden rule is to remember the probability of spelling discrepancies: dropped Hs and misinterpreted letters.

The law stated that children were to be registered within forty-two days of their birth, but you may find some births missing in the early years, since there was no mechanism in place to make sure a child had been registered. A lot of poorer people, who could be distrustful of any government form, did not bother. But an Act passed in 1872 meant that the person present at the birth (e.g. the midwife) had a responsibility to inform the registrar. The registrar would then impose a fine of £2 on the parents if the child was not registered. This meant, however, that sometimes an incorrect birth date was given in order to avoid a late registration fee.

While searching down the lists of names on the birth indexes you will notice that sometimes the words 'male' or 'female' are added at the end of each surname section. It seems that our ancestors found it difficult to decide upon the child's name, so if a name still wasn't decided when it came time to register the birth, they would just tell the registrar if the child was a boy or a girl. Another reason for this could have been the high infant mortality rate; not naming a baby until they were sure it was healthy.

A birth certificate will give you the date and place of birth; the place is often just the name of the parish and not necessarily a full address. It will tell you the father's name and his occupation, and the mother's name, including her maiden name. If the mother had been married before it is usual for all three names to be given. In the case of an illegitimate birth the box for the 'name and surname of father' is often left blank. But be warned: before 1875 the mother could give any name she wished; she could even pretend to be married, as no proof was asked for. By 1874 an act had been passed which stated that from January 1875, the father of an illegitimate child had to be present at the registration of the birth in order for his name to appear on the birth certificate.

Marriages were registered by the person who performed the ceremony, so unless a couple had very common names and married miles from home, it is very likely you will find a marriage. Yet it could be possible, in very rare cases, that the couple did not marry at all, even in those days, and so it is known for a marriage not to be found.

A marriage certificate will give you the date and the place the marriage took place, be it a church, chapel or the register office. In some cases it will give you the exact ages of the bride and groom. In others, more so in earlier marriages, it may only tell you that they were either 'of full age' or a 'minor'. It will tell you whether they were both single, or had been widowed or divorced (although divorce was rare, and usually only happened among the wealthier classes). It will give you an occupation and where the parties were living at the time of the marriage. It will also give you the fathers' names and their occupations. Yet some illegitimate people, when being married, were known to invent a father's name or even give their grandfather's name. Occasionally a father would be deceased, but the registrar was not informed; leading to difficulties when looking for a person's date of death. You will see if the couple signed their names or 'made their mark' and who witnessed the wedding. Witnesses at a wedding can be an important clue – they may be other family members – a brother or sister, perhaps even an uncle or aunt.

As a burial could not take place unless a death certificate was produced, it is likewise unusual not to find the death of an ancestor. Although in some cases it can be a lengthy search if you are unsure of the year, and problems can arise if someone died a long way from home and their certificate is hidden amongst numerous deaths all over the country.

It is probably for these reasons that a lot of people tend to only get birth and marriage certificates, particularly as these do help to continue their research. If they need the mother's maiden name some researchers buy a child's birth certificate; if they need to know a father's name, a marriage certificate can be obtained. But sometimes people just don't bother with death certificates; if they've found the burial, then they know to within a few days when a person died. Even sometimes just knowing the year and quarter will be satisfactory. But, as morbid as it seems, it can be interesting to know what your ancestor died from.

There are many causes of death which are now not used in modern day medical terms, one example being 'senile' or 'natural' decay. This basically meant old age, and it seems this satisfactorily covered the death of many an old person. Disease of the heart would cover all types of heart attack and a stroke is often referred to as 'palsy'.

Searching the GRO indexes for a death before the March quarter of 1866 can be difficult because you are only given a name and the registration district. From January 1866 the age of the deceased was added to the index, which does at least narrow the search down. Although the age at death did not appear on the indexes before 1866, it does appear on the actual death certificate. From the June quarter of 1969 the age was changed to the inclusion of a date of birth.

Between 1837 and 1969 the format of a death certificate, however, remained the same. You will get the date and place the person died, the age of that person, and the cause of death. If a man, his occupation will be given; if a married woman, her husband's name. She will be stated as being either 'wife of' or 'widow of' which will give you a clue as to her husband's date of death. The informant's name, address and relationship to the deceased can, of course, be useful; it may be a married daughter whom you didn't know was married. The informant may be a coroner, therefore prompting a search in the newspapers to find the circumstances of the death.

From 1969 the date and place of birth is included and, in the case of a married woman, the maiden name. Birth and marriage certificates have remained standard since 1837.

When talking of births it is necessary to mention adoption. Unfortunately, before 1927 there was no formal adoption process; a child would just be given away, its name changed, and, unless it had kept its original birth certificate, it became impossible for its descendants to know who gave birth to the child. Tracing the ancestry of an adopted child after 1927 can also be difficult as a strict code of secrecy shields the identity of the child's biological family. An adoption certificate will only give the adoptive parents' names – not those of the birth mother or father, although the child can apply to the courts for its own original birth certificate. In most cases the children of that child can also apply, but the authorities always ask that legal advice should be sought. At present there seems to be no assistance for those just wanting to trace their family trees which seems a great pity when so many people find this such an absorbing hobby.

Census Records

Imagine you have an ancestor who was born in 1840 and died in 1912. You now have the opportunity to follow his life through at ten year intervals. First he is a baby living with his parents, and perhaps siblings. Ten years later there are more siblings. Perhaps his mother has died (a common occurrence in families due to the hazardous nature of childbirth) and he has a stepmother. Ten years later again and he is now nearly 21. He will be employed himself – perhaps he is lodging with his employer, perhaps he has moved away from his hometown. At 30 he is probably married with children of his own. Perhaps he has bettered himself; where before he was a farm labourer, perhaps now he has a farm of his own; he may have been an apprentice shoemaker, but now he is a master shoemaker. Twenty or thirty years later he may have married children living with him, with their children. By the time he is 70 he may be living with one of his children, and miles away from his place of birth.

The census was taken every ten years around March or April, apart from in 1841, when it was taken in June. The exact dates are:

1841 – 7 June	1881 – 4 April
1851 – 31 March	1891 – 6 April
1861 – 8 April	1901 – 1 April
1871 – 3 April	1911 – 2 April

Page from the 1841 census of North & Middle Littleton. Ref: HO107/1191/10/4.
(Courtesy of Worcester Register Office)

There were headcounts taken in previous decades from 1801, by the 'overseers of the poor' and other officials – but the majority of these have not survived, and are of limited use to the family historian in any case.

The first census of any real use is that taken in 1841. From 1841 it was the duty of the local registrar to arrange the census and he employed a local enumerator who walked from house to house handing out the census forms. These were then collected and the details added to the enumerator's book, which was then passed to the registrar. Each enumerator started his book with a description of where he had walked, which can be useful, as addresses were not always entered in their entirety. With small villages just the village name would suffice.

A typical description, taken from 1851, Inkberrow, is as follows:

All that part of the parish of Inkberrow comprising the whole of Egiock Lane to the top. The whole of the Ridgway, right and left from the top of Egiock Lane to the top of Cladswell Lane to Dogbut Farm.

Following the route on a map, going from household to household, will give you an idea of where your ancestor was living. This page will also give you the registration district. In this instance it is Alcester.

The 1841 census does have less information than those of the following decades, but can still be helpful when investigating where a family was, and who was living with the family or was still alive. What it will not do is tell you the place of birth. The question 'were you born in this county?' was asked, therefore it will be a yes or no. If it is 'yes' then at least you know you're still in the right county, but a 'no' can mean a very long search or perhaps the worst situation of all: the proverbial brick wall. Ages are also rounded to the nearest five for adults over 14, making it difficult to establish an exact date of birth. Nor were relationships included, so it can only be assumed that children living in the household were sons and daughters, but it could be that they were nephews or nieces. Older residents living with the family could be parents, but then again they could be uncles or aunts, or even older siblings.

A household group will be divided between non-family members by an oblique (/). Individual households are divided by a double oblique.

Beginning with the census of 1851, the exact place of birth was asked and exact ages were given (as exact as we can expect from our ancestors). The relationship to the head of the house was given as was the 'condition', meaning marital status. There was also a column for stating whether the person was blind or deaf and dumb. In 1871 the words imbecile, idiot or lunatic were added to this column, and by 1891 a column for stating how many rooms were occupied and whether the person was an employer or employee was introduced. In 1901 this also included whether a person was working at home.

But, as mentioned before, don't always rely on the information shown being accurate. In some cases the poorer people distrusted anything the government introduced, so purposefully withheld or gave misleading information. Sometimes they simply couldn't answer the questions. For example, they may not have known where they were born. They could have grown up in a parish as a child and not realised they had been born somewhere else and that the family had moved away when they were babies.

Page from the 1851 census of Kidderminster. Ref: HO107/2038/601/7. (Courtesy of Worcester Register Office)

It has already been noted how there can be discrepancies in ages and these are most noticeable in the census. You may see a difference of eight years rather than ten between the years of the census. This can sometimes be due to our ancestors not knowing how old they really were. How many people celebrated birthdays in those days? If they didn't then what record would they have, the older they got? If they couldn't read, their birth certificate would be of no use to them, moreover they may have been born before civil registration began.

In large towns, like Worcester itself, you will find streets are split between different enumeration districts. If you know an ancestor lived in a certain street make sure you have covered the whole of it. There are street indexes in Worcester Family History Centre for the larger towns, so you can see where each division of a street appears on each roll of film. Of course, if you use an Internet site like Ancestry or Findmypast you can search the name index which will take you straight to a particular family. However, you have to be aware of not only the spelling discrepancy made by the enumerator on the original form, but the spelling discrepancies made by the people indexing the pages who found it difficult to read the handwriting.

One such example involves the surname Keyte. Searching an index for a family with this name produced a different spelling for four censuses. In one census it was correctly spelt as Keyte, on another as Prayte, then Sheybe and then, curiously, Brookes. With both the Prayte and Sheybe spelling it was quite obvious looking at the original how this had happened. The 'K' did resemble 'Pr' and the 'e' could have been an 'a'. Then another year the 'K' did seem to be 'Sh' and the 't' appeared to be a 'b'. More unusually, but worth bearing in mind; in a further instance the Keytes had been mixed up with their neighbours and appeared in the index as Brookes', although in this case the name was written quite clearly as Keyte.

If these problems occur it is often a good idea to just put in a christian name, age and place of birth, and to go through all those which are listed looking at all the odd spellings.

However christian names can also be spelt in unusual ways. Sometimes Thomas was abbreviated to 'Thos.', William to 'Wllm.' and Samuel to 'Saml.' and this is how they have also been presented on the index. In these cases the wildcard (★) comes in useful. For example if you type 'Sam★' all variations will be shown such as Sam, Samuel, Saml etc.

Page from the 1901 census of Feckenham. Ref. RG13/2943/12/16. (Courtesy of Worcester Register Office)

Furthermore, it was not unusual for middle names to be used rather than a first name, or they may have swapped them round. One year a John Henry may be found as John Henry or John H. Another he may be Henry John or Henry J. Another year he may simply be known as Harry. It was quite common for a middle name to be used instead of the first name.

At present the 1911 census is only available on the Internet and only at the Findmypast site. When you look at this census you will find it totally different to any of the previous censuses, although it is likely that you will refer to this census first and thus find all the others to be different. Here we are shown the original form that our ancestor filled in, and the additional information it gives us will prove to be invaluable in your research. The head and his wife had to state how many years they had been married. They were also asked to fill in the number of children they had had, and how many were still living or had died. Other information asked was what industry they were involved in, for example, if they gave their occupation as 'press hand' they would then state that they were employed at a brick works.

As the 1911 census was made available before the usual 100-year disclosure period had elapsed, sensitive information has been redacted. This includes information on whether a person had any disability, be it physical or mental.

The census is perhaps one of the best tools for the family historian, but do not gloss over any unusual circumstances you notice within a family unit. If you see a very young child with parents you feel could be too old to have conceived, look at the older children. Is there a daughter of childbearing age? Very often when a young daughter gave birth to an illegitimate baby her parents brought it up as their own. Do not always assume that the wife of the head of the household is the mother of your ancestor. For example, you may go back to the previous census, ten years earlier, and find that your great great-great-grandfather has a different wife. Childbirth meant high mortality rates among women, and men married again quickly if there was a young family to be looked after.

You may see many unusual occupations listed in the census. These can be seen in parish registers and on certificates, too. For example, a cordwainer was the name given to a shoemaker; an annuitant is someone receiving an income from a source other than an employer. In the needle industry of the Redditch district, an eyer was someone who made the eyes in needles; a pointer someone who filed and sharpened needles. In the silk industry of Blockley, a dresser was someone who prepared the silk for weaving; whilst a throwster twisted the silk into thread or yarn. A twister was another name for spinner; an engine turner turned the wheel on weaving looms. Around the borders of Birmingham you may find a japanner, this was a specialised industry which used the Japanese lacquering process in varnishing.

Other examples include the cabman, who drove small horse drawn passenger vehicles whereas a carman, who drove a vehicle used to transport goods, could also be known as a carrier or carter. A stationary engine driver operated machinery in a factory, mill or mine; a striker was a blacksmith's assistant. A chandler could be one of two occupations; a candle maker or seller of candles or sometimes a grocer. A malster worked in the brewing industry and a victualler sold food or drink. If someone was referred to as 'jobbing' he was employed on a casual basis. In the mining districts a hewer was the miner who worked underground digging out the coal, whereas a banksman worked at the surface.

An easy mistake made due to the handwriting of the day, with 'l' and 's' being very similar, are the very different occupations of lawyer and sawyer. You may be disappointed to find that the ancestor you thought to be a distinguished servant of legal system was, in fact, a woodman. Likewise, a yeoman is often mistaken for a soldier of some kind but is actually a term for a freeholder, which was considered the next class down from gentry.

So enjoy taking the streets the enumerator took and meeting your ancestors and their neighbours, but always allow for their little indiscretions.

Inside the Parish

For our ancestors the parish church was the centre of their communities and lives. It was where they went to get married, to baptise their children and to be buried. They met their friends there on a Sunday and sometimes they went there cap in hand to ask for financial assistance. There are many records associated with the church where a family historian can find a wealth of information, not just about his own ancestor, but about their neighbours and the community in general.

Almost every parish in Worcestershire was controlled by the diocese of Worcester. However, the Worcester diocese expanded beyond the borders of the county and therefore included parishes in Warwickshire, too. Equally you will find a small corner of Worcestershire – east of Clifton-on-Teme, Abberley and Bewdley to the Herefordshire border town of Tenbury – which belongs to the diocese of Hereford.

For this reason, when searching for documents pertaining to the diocese rather than the county (i.e. wills, marriage bonds and allegations) you can find information on families from parishes in Warwickshire, too. Parishes starting at Tanworth and extending south through Studley, Wooton Wawen, Snitterfield, Wellesbourne, Brailes to Whichford and the Comptons belong to the diocese of Worcester – so their records belonging to the diocese can be found in Worcester Family History Centre.

There are maps in Worcester Family History Centre which detail the parishes within the Worcester diocese. However, there are a few parishes which fall under the category 'peculiars'. Peculiars are parishes which do not come under the jurisdiction of the bishop, but a dean or chapter, or the church's own incumbent and, in some cases, the Crown. The Worcestershire peculiars are Alvechurch, Berrow, Bredon, Fladbury & Throckmorton, Hanbury, Hartlebury, Kempsey, Norton, Ripple, Stock & Bradley, Stoulton, Tibberton, Tredington, Wolverley and Worcester St Michael.

It is also necessary to be aware that some places which fall on the county borders may only be half in the county, notably Dudley, which is divided between Worcestershire and Staffordshire. For this reason not every record, document or register can be found in Worcester Family History Centre or Record Office. Many are kept at the Dudley Record Office in Coseley.

Parish Registers

There are over 300 parishes in Worcestershire and microfilms of their registers are all held at Worcester Family History Centre. Some parish's volumes date back to the time register-keeping first began in the mid-1500s and cover 400 years, taking a parish into the 1900s, even as far as the 1960s and the 1980s.

Thomas Cromwell passed a law in 1538 that registers of baptisms, burials and marriages were to be kept. These early registers were only written on paper until 1598, so not many from before 1598 have survived. After 1598 the registers were made of parchment and at that time the clergy were ordered to copy entries on to parchment for those entries belonging to Queen Elizabeth's reign, so some records do go back to 1558.

Before 1754 parish registers were kept in various books at the discretion of the vicar. All the books were blank-paged volumes and the vicar wrote down exactly what he wanted to – some were more forthcoming than others. The child's name and its parents' names were given on baptism registers, but some vicars may have also added the place they lived, or the occupation of the father. Whilst one vicar may have only put the deceased's name in the burial registers, another may have included an age, another still the parents' names if the burial was that of a child.

Sometimes all the baptisms, marriages and burials can be found written together, in chronological order, but in other cases the vicar was more meticulous and split the register into three sections, thus listing the three events separately. Still others recorded just the marriages separately but put the baptisms and burials together. This can be useful when building up a picture of a family group as you can not only find the children who were baptised in that particular family group but also those who died in infancy. But even when the baptism and burials are separated you can sometimes spot the death of a child. Parents often re-used names so you will often find a child who had been given the name of a deceased older sibling. This is something to watch out for when searching for the baptism of a direct ancestor. If you find a baptism that does not fit with the date you had expected, check the burials. You may find this child had died and your ancestor was baptised a short while later and given his deceased brother's name. You may even find your ancestor actually had different parents; had you jumped at the first entry, you would have found yourself climbing up the wrong tree. So never assume you have found the correct entry and always do a little more research. The same applies when you find two baptisms of the name you are looking for, but with different parents' names. Check the burials because if one has died, and the parents' names are included on the burial entry, one will be eliminated and you will know which is yours.

Between 1666 and 1814 you may see written in a burial registers 'buried in woollen'. This was due to an act which had been introduced to help the wool trade. There were fines for those who did not comply. During the years of the Commonwealth (1649–60), when many parish priests were evicted from their churches by the Puritans, the parish registers were not always kept. Sometimes you may find births entered rather than baptisms and sometimes events were listed later, after the Restoration.

A significant reform to affect the parish registers was the change from the Julian calendar to the Gregorian calendar in 1752. Prior to 1752 England was still using the Julian calendar, in which the New Year began on 25 March. The Gregorian calendar, which had been introduced by Pope

Examples of baptisms, marriages and burials taken from Beoley Parish Registers by kind permission of David Rogers, rector of St Leonards, Beoley. A page from the sixteenth century *(Left)* and the seventeenth century *(Right)* shows baptisms, marriages and burials together on same page. Not all registers from this era are of such good quality; an example such as this must still be scrutinised closely as the handwriting is so different from the modern-day.

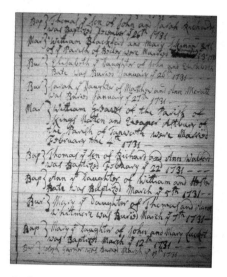

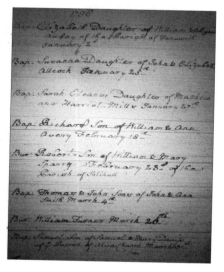

(Left) A page from the eighteenth century shows baptisms, burials and marriages (up to 1754) on the same page. *(Right)* A page from the nineteenth century shows baptisms and burials on the same page.

The marriage register after 1754.

The baptism register after 1813.

The burials register after 1813.

The marriage register after 1837.

Gregory XVIII in 1582, had now spread across Europe so England followed suit. However, to match dates on the continent it was necessary for us to lose eleven days and the dates 3–13 September disappeared from the year of 1752. This means that when you see a baptism dated 3 February 1749 it could be said to have taken place in 1750.

The next change came with the Hardwicke's Marriage Act of 1754. This stated that a marriage had to take place in an Anglican church, in either the groom's or the bride's parish, with two witnesses present. The banns were to be read on three consecutive Sundays in both the groom and bride's parish, if they came from different parishes. The reading of banns was not a new event, but it had not previously been law, and couples could marry without them in any parish they chose. Only Jews and Quakers were exempt from the Hardwicke Act.

Special registers were produced which the clergy were under obligation to complete, although not all were filled in accurately. They would give the names of the groom and bride, the parish in which they lived, whether the man was a bachelor and the woman a spinster, or if either of them was widowed. They would sign the register, or make their mark – usually with a cross. The two witnesses would also sign or make their mark. Very often you will see the same witness at numerous marriages. This was often one of the church wardens who stood in as a witness.

Rose's Act of 1812 introduced special books for baptisms and burials from 1813. Again these were pre-printed with columns which had to be filled in by the vicar or curate or one of the church wardens. A baptism register includes the date, the child's name, the parent's names, place of abode and occupation of the father. The burial register gives the deceased's name, place of abode, age and date of burial. Both these styles have continued to the present day.

When civil registration began in 1837 the marriage register also changed to become a duplicate of the certificate held at the register office. Now a couple could marry in the register office instead if in a church.

In certain circumstances the couple took out a marriage licence. After the Hardwick's Marriage Act, when all marriages had to take place in the parish church, a licence was often a way to avoid the reading of banns if the parties were non-conformists. Taking out a licence also meant the marriage could take place without the three-week wait for the banns to be read, so often it might mean there was a sense of urgency to the marriage. There was a fee to take out a licence so it was usually only the upper classes which went for this option, and often as a status symbol rather than as a necessity.

The relevant Bond and Allegation would be kept by the diocese and Worcester Family History Centre holds those for the diocese of Worcester. A bond and allegation should be found a few days prior to the marriage. The groom and his bondsman (e.g. 'William Oakley of the parish of Claines, groom, and Samuel Oakley of Grimley, labourer') would appear before the office of the Bishop of Worcester and swear that:

> William Oakley a widower and Mary Tague a widow may lawfully solemnize marriage together.

Ages would be given but as the term 'and upward' follows the age it can't always be taken as being exact. In this case, William was aged 30 and upward and Mary Tague 21 years and upward. The marriage took place at Claines on 1 March 1802.

It may be a surprise to learn that, before the Marriage Act of 1929, the minimum legal age for marriage was 14 years for a boy and 12 years for a girl, although in most cases it was unusual for people to marry at those young ages. The Age of Marriage Act 1929 raised this age to 16 years for both parties.

To help find a baptism or marriage in the parish registers you can consult the International Genealogical Index (IGI). The IGI is produced by the Church of the Latter Day Saints. An early version is available on microfiche in Worcester Family History Centre, and updated versions can be found at www.familysearch.org. Once again one must remember to allow for human error and every entry extracted from the IGI should be checked on the original parish register. The IGI also only gives dates, places and names so checking the original page will give you additional information, particularly after 1754 for marriages, and 1813 for baptisms. As it is not a complete index, if you do not find an entry it does not necessarily mean the event did not happen, so you must still search the appropriate parish register.

There is a marriage index in Worcester Family History Centre which you will find very helpful. For the grooms' names it covers 1660–1837, and for the brides' 1701–1837. It is split into five sections with regards to the grooms' names: 1660–1700, 1701–1754, 1755–1800 and 1801–1837. The surnames are listed alphabetically and give the bride's name, the date and the parish in which the marriage took place. You can then go straight to that register to check for the full details. The brides' index covers the whole period of 1701–1837 with the surnames and christian names being listed alphabetically. As with the men's index, the spouse's name, date and parish are included, but the marriages are not given in date order.

Some vicars could be quite eloquent and you may see interesting notes made by the vicar such as this entry made in 1686 in the Rushock register:

Elizabeth Waldron was borne upon a Friday. She caught ye Smallpox at Stourbridge upon a Friday, fell ill the Friday following ... and dyed upon the Good Friday ... and was buried at Ribbesford in ye Rectors Chancell upon Easter Day April 4th.

In Stoke Prior on 13 July 1748 a baptism reads:

John the son of Elizabeth Laugher – illegitimately begotten by her brother-in-law John Laugher (vile dog).

At Upper Arley on 29 April 1742 the baptism took place of:

Joseph an illegitimate child nursed by Margaret the wife of William Farmer who says she does not know the mother, but that he was born in the parish of Kidderminster.

Sometimes notes written by the vicar can lead to further research. One attached to an ancestor's records can add an interesting story. In the burial register for Birtsmorton is an entry which reads:

May 11th 1780. Thomas Sheen of Castlemorton who was murdered with three others in Berrow parish in a most inhuman and barbarous manner.

If Thomas belongs in your tree your natural curiosity could take you on an interesting journey through the newspapers of the day. It will tell you that Thomas was murdered together with his sister-in-law, Elizabeth Gummery, her husband Edward and their daughter Ann. All had been hacked to death and the scene described in the newspaper gives a vivid description of bowels hanging out, limbs severed and throats cut!

Or you may discover an ancestor with a sad past. Charles Duffin was buried at Alvechurch on 2 September 1873 and a note has been added to the register saying 'suicide, temporary insanity'. Unfortunately, there are no coroner reports available for Worcestershire; however a look at the local paper, the *Bromsgrove, Droitwich and Redditch Weekly Messenger* for Saturday, 6 September 1873 reveals an account of the inquest:

ALVECHURCH. SUICIDE. Unhappily of late the occurrence of sudden deaths, either by the visitation of God or self-destruction, is by no means rare in this neighbourhood. In this issue we are called upon to chronicle the proceedings of an inquest held on Monday Evening last by R. Docker esq., Coroner, at the Red Lion Inn, on the body of Charles Dufffin, labourer, aged about forty years, a native of this district. The evidence forth coming showed that on Saturday last the body of the deceased was found in a shed by Ernest Fisher, son of Mr Geo. Fisher, labourer, of Longfield, to whom the shed belonged; and it appeared that Duffin had been sleeping in the building, which is not far from Mr Fisher's residence, for a short time. Deceased employed for his destruction a piece of cord, taken from a drill in that place, which he fastened to one of the rafters, and it was evident that the cord broke before life was extinct, as the corpse was lying partially in the manger, with a portion of the rope around the neck. There was also a wound on the back of the head and marks of blood on the wall occasioned by the fall, and, judging from appearances, the fatal fall act must have been committed several days before it was discovered. A verdict of 'Suicide whilst in a state of temporary insanity' was given by the jury. The body was interred in the graveyard early on Tuesday morning.

The registers for baptisms, marriages and burials are not the only parish records to be found. There are many documents which can put flesh on the bones; records which can give you an insight into how your ancestors may have lived or life in the parish which they lived. Unfortunately, unlike the parish registers, not all these books and documents have survived the test of time. A lot were inadvertently destroyed by people feeling the need to tidy the church, or they were moved elsewhere and have eventually got lost. But if you can find any of these records they can be very interesting to read and in some cases they can help you trace back through further generations.

Poor Law Records

The Poor Law was in operation between 1601 and 1834. Parish officials known as the overseers of the poor were elected each year to hold meetings, hand out assistance and make numerous decisions regarding the running of the parish. The sort of records you can find here are Vestry Meeting Minutes, Settlements and Removals, Apprenticeship Indentures, Bastardy Bonds and Church Wardens' Accounts. Some are on microfilm at Worcester Family History Centre and can be found at the end of all the baptisms, marriage and burial registers, but most are held in their original form at the Record Office at County Hall up at Spetchley on the outskirts of Worcester. They can be found, if they have survived, by searching the Bulk Accessions (BAs) card indexes at either the Record Office or Worcester Family History Centre. There are catalogued under either the specific parish as 'poor law records' or 'overseers of the poor', or in the box for the Ps under the word 'poor'.

Vestry Meetings

If a parishioner fell on hard times they would go cap in hand to the church to ask for assistance, or relief, as it was then known. Regular vestry meetings were held for these purposes and in some parishes articulate books were kept of the meetings. The parishioners did not always get what they wanted, and going through the books you often see the same names over and over again.

For example in the parish of Feckenham the Pierce, Wells and Chatterley families are regularly making appearances:

7 November 1821	William Chatterley applies for relief – allowed 1s. per week.
21 November 1821	William Chatterley applies for some more relief – not allowed.
7 August 1822	William Chatterley's pay of 1s. per week to be stopped.
3 September 1823	William Chatterley apples for 4d towards a bed – allowed.
5 November 1823	George Wells applies for linen for a pair of sheets and a shirt. Allowed a shirt.
3 March 1824	William Pierce's wife applies for clothing – not allowed.
1 November 1826	William Pierce's wife applies for 2s per week during the winter and also a pair of shoes. Allowed a pair of shoes.
5 December 1827	George Wells applies for linen for children and shoes for him and his wife. Allowed linen.
7 May 1828	George Wells. Pay his rent. Allowed one pound towards it.
6 August 1828	George Wells wife applies for money to redeem their goods seized for rent. Allowed 1 pound. William Chatterley applies for a further allowance a week. Able to get 2/6 per week if he had work. Allowed 3s. a week till he can do without it.
5 November 1828	William Pierce's wife applies for a pair of shoes. Allowed 4s towards them.
7 July 1830	William Chatterley applies for money towards paying his doctors. Allowed 6d more per week.

3 November 1830	John Pierce's wife applies for linen for children. Allowed 4 yards calico.
5 January 1831	George Wells applies for his shoes to be mended and a new frock. Shoes mended and frock allowed. John Chatterley applies for a blanket and a shirt. Allowed.
4 May 1831	Joseph Chatterley's wife applies for relief for her daughter. And Linen. Allowed occasional relief.
1 June 1831	Joseph Chatterley applies for more relief for his daughter. Allowed. Joseph Pierce applies for a shirt. Allowed.
3 August 1831	Joseph Pierce applies for more relief. Not allowed.
7 September 1831	Joseph Pierce applies for more weekly pay. Not allowed.
2 November 1831	George Wells applies for shoes. Allowed 5s. towards a pair.

The money handed out to the poor was raised through the poor rate or church rate and was imposed on the occupier of a house or land in the parish. It was collected by the churchwardens, and the amount was set out annually at the vestry meeting each Easter. Problems occurred from the 1830s due to non-conformists not wanting to pay taxes to the parish church, and the poor rate was abolished in 1868.

If you want to find out the equivalent in today's currency of how much these people were given, there is a conversion link on the National Archives website.

Settlements and Removals

If an ancestor died before the census was first taken and there is no record of him in the baptisms of the parish he was living or married in, it is likely that he moved into the parish from elsewhere. For this problem a settlement examination or certificate is invaluable. If someone was moving from one parish to another parish it was usually necessary for them to take out a legal settlement, so that if they required relief, the overseers would know who was responsible for them.

They would present themselves before the overseers where they would have to give evidence of where they were born and all their movements from that time up to their arrival in this particular parish. If you are lucky enough to find one of these you can trace an ancestor's working life, as well as knowing where to look for their baptism and those of their parents.

A person could claim legal settlement of a parish if they:

- Rented property of £10 per annum;
- Had worked in the parish for a year;
- Were the wife of a man from the parish;
- Were an legitimate child, aged 7 or under, whose father lived in the parish;
- Were an illegitimate child born in the parish;
- Were an apprentice hired by a parishioner;
- Paid parish rate or were a parish official;
- Had lived in the parish for forty days and given written notice of their intention to do so.

People entering a parish with the intent of living there would be examined by the justices of the peace in order for their place of legal settlement to be ascertained. Settlement examinations can vary in length according to the number of places the person had lived and worked. For example, a short one will state where the person was born, that he had moved in to the parish when he was an apprentice, and now wanted to settle there. Another may show that the person had travelled and worked in many parishes.

One such case, from December 1831, is worth quoting in full. William Parsonage had to give an account of his legal place of settlement when living in Feckenham. His settlement examination showed he had been born in Northfield but:

when very young [he] went with his father and mother into the parish of Kings Norton. When about 15 years of age he was hired to a Mr Hicklin a farmer in the same parish of Kings Norton for a year which he served and was then hired again for another year and served his master Hicklin three years in the same parish. He was then hired by Mr Parkes of the parish of

Alvechurch farmer for one at the wages of six pounds ten shillings and served his whole year. He was then hired by Mr John Brettell of the parish of Kings Norton farmer for a year at the wages of seven pounds – he was then hired by Mr Abraham Onions of the parish of Tadebigge for a year at the wages of nine pounds that he served his year and then was hired again and served Mr Onions two years longer in the same parish – that he married his present wife Sarah by whom he has four children namely Mary Ann aged about 11 years, Sarah aged about 9, William aged about 5 and John aged about 2 years – that about one year and a half after his marriage he rented a house, outbuildings and about 4 acres of land of George Albutt of the parish of Feckenham farmer for one year at the rent of £12 – that he then went to Birmingham and worked at weekly wages for about four years and then about two years ago last michaelmas went and took a house outbuildings and about ten acres of land of a Mr William Cheshire in the parish of Arley in the county of Warwick for a year – that he lived on this estate for about six months only namely from michaelmas to lady day when John Cheshire brother of the said William Cheshire came and demanded the rent saying the place belonged to him and said he had better leave it for it would never do him any good. The examinant paid half year's rent of £10 and soon afterwards left on being paid for seed and labour on the land and that on ladyday last he took a house outbuildings and land in the parish of Feckenham of Thomas Green blacksmith for one years rent of £13 and has paid £6 10s the half years rent due at michaelmas last.

It has been mentioned that our ancestors did a lot more moving about than we may think. At a rough estimation, during those years, William had travelled over 100 miles. Northfield to Kings Norton is about 2 miles; Kings Norton to Alvechurch, 5 miles; then another 5 miles back to Kings Norton. Kings Norton to Tardebigge is 12 miles; Tardebigge to Feckenham, 10 miles; and Feckenham to Birmingham, 22 miles. He then went from Birmingham to Arley which is about 18 miles; and Arley to Feckenham is 38 miles. That makes approximately 112 miles. It may not sound a lot by today's standards but in the 1820s, probably travelling by foot most of the time, with young children, it would have been a difficult journey.

Sometimes settlement examinations can give details of where other family members may have lived. For instance, in October 1835 a widow by the name of Sarah Lea was examined in Feckenham. She said she had been born in Eckington but had married thirty years earlier to John Lea of Feckenham, who had died four months earlier. But she went on to say that her father-in-law was of the parish of Wootton Wawen in Warwickshire and had received relief from that parish, and that when he died his wife had continued to receive relief for about five or six years. If John Lea were your ancestor, you would now know it to be likely that his baptism had been in Wootton Wawen and that when you find his father's burial, it is likely his mother's will be five or six years later. Sarah and John's marriage will probably be found in Feckenham, as it appears John had already left his family's home and settled in Feckenham.

If a person, or family, did fall on hard times and needed relief, but had not taken out a legal settlement, the churchwardens and overseers could make a complaint to the justices of the peace. A retrospective settlement examination would be arranged and a decision would then be made as to what would happen to the family. In all probability a removal order would be issued to send them back to where was considered their legal place of settlement. The offending parties would then be escorted back to the parish boundary by a constable, together with a copy of the removal order. A family historian has the advantage of searching both parishes; the parish the person is being removed from and the parish considered to be their legal place of settlement.

An example of a typical Removal Order reads as follows:

Whereas complaint hath been made by you the Churchwardens and overseers of the Poor of the parish of Birmingham unto us whose hands and seals are here unto set, two of his Majesties Justices of the Peace for the County of Warwickshire that Richard Rowley labourer lately intruded himself into the said parish of Birmingham there to inhabit as your parishioner, contrary to the laws relating to the settlement of the poor and is chargeable to the parish of Birmingham.

We, upon examining, Richard Rowley upon oath touching his settlement do adjudge the premises to be true and that the last place of legal settlement of the said Richard Rowley is in the parish of Astley

The order then instructed the Birmingham churchwardens or overseers to:

remove and convey the said Richard Rowley from your said parish of Birmingham to the said parish of Astley and him deliver to the Churchwardens and Overseers of the Poor there, together with this our warrant or Order, or a true copy thereof.

This would have been the order, or copy, which Richard Rowley, brought back with him. Others in this bundle were orders taken out by the churchwardens of Astley to have someone removed back to another parish.

Apprenticeship Indentures

Apprenticeship indentures can show you the dire financial straits some families could find themselves in. If parents could not afford to look after their children, rather than give the family relief, the overseers of the poor would hand a child over as an apprentice to any one who was willing to take them on. A child as young as 7 could be handed over, and sometimes these masters could live miles from the child's home. In fact, masters were often sought in neighbouring parishes as once a child had served forty days as an apprentice, they then had a right of settlement in that parish. This meant that their home parish was relieved of ever having to provide relief for the child. An apprenticeship could last seven years or until the child reached the age of 21, and apprentices were not allowed to marry without their master's consent. You will see entries in the vestry meeting minutes of the decisions to send particular children out as apprentices, and the church warden's accounts will show the amount a master was paid to take a child as an apprentice.

The indentures suggest the apprentice was going to be trained in some kind of trade in return for their keep, but very often they were just used as cheap labour, sometimes sleeping in cramped conditions with little food.

Apprenticeship indentures were standard documents filled in by the churchwardens and the overseers of the poor.

The trade description of husbandry or housewifery was sometimes simply a cover for the master to gain a cheap servant. Once the children were placed as an apprentice there was no check to make sure they were being looked after, and masters considered apprentices to be their property. If a child did run away a reward was offered for its return. You will often see notices, such as the following from 1743, in a local newspaper:

> Went away from his master Mr Richard Lakin, shoemaker in Moor Street, on Saturday the 24th August John Brown about 19 years of age, lame on his right side, fresh-coloured with straight hair, had on when he went away a brown cape coat, with yellow buttons and has just one year to serve. This is to forewarn all persons from employing him and to desire any who may know where he is to inform the said master and they shall receive all reasonable charges.

Finding an indenture could tell you whether your ancestor was rich or poor. If your ancestor was a master then he was probably quite comfortable financially, and searching through the indentures may show that he became the master of several apprentices. Alternatively, you may find the majority of your ancestor's siblings were also sent out as apprentices. Some on the same day; all to different places. Whole families could be split up at the direction of the overseers. A typical apprenticeship indenture reads:

> That (names) Churchwardens of the parish of (name) and Overseers of the Poor of the said parish by and with the consent of his Majesties' Justices of the Peace do put and place (name) aged (age) or thereabouts, a poor child of the said parish, Apprentice to (name) in the said parish of (name) with him to dwell and serve from the Day of the Date of these Presents, until the said apprentice shall accomplish his/her full Age of Twenty One Years or until the Day of Marriage.
>
> During all which Term the said apprentice his/her master faithfully shall serve in all lawful business according to his/her power wit and ability and honestly orderly and obediently in all things demean and behalf him/herself towards his/her said master and his during his/her said term.
>
> [The master] shall and will teach and instruct or cause to be taught and instructed in the best way and manner he can. And shall and will during all the term find and provide and allow sufficient meat, drink, apparel, lodging, washing and other things necessary and fit for an apprentice.

There was also an agreement that if the master died the apprentice would be transferred to the executors as part of the estate. This last clause really does show that the apprentice was considered the property of the Master, no different than a piece of furniture.

Bastardy Bonds

If an unmarried woman found she was expecting a child she could appear before the parish and a bastardy certificate was taken out, thus ensuring the man responsible could pay his way rather than the parish having to provide for the child and its mother. However if your ancestor was illegitimate you may not find one of these bonds. More often than not the father went undetected. The following example is from 21 December 1765:

> Know all men by these presents that I William Dickens of Lower Astley in the county of Worcester, yeoman, am held and firmly bound to Thomas Griffin churchwarden and William Pastons overseer of the poor of the parish of Astley in the same county in forty pounds of lawful money to be paid to the churchwardens and overseers.
>
> Whereas Mary Rutter singlewoman hath been lately delivered of a female bastard child likely to become chargeable to the said parish of Astley and hath duly charged the above bound William Dickens with being the father of the said child.

> Now the condition of the above obligation is such that if the above bound William Dickens, his heirs, exors or admons do and shall from time to time and at all times hereafter fully and wholly indemnify.

Overseers' Accounts

The overseers' accounts give a record of what was handed out as agreed in the vestry meeting. If the minutes you are after have not survived, you may still be able to see if your ancestor needed any relief.

Although usually not as detailed as the minutes – only giving the name and amount – occasionally there may be a little information. The Feckenham overseer's accounts from 1813 list a few explanations:

Edward Waine, lame hand.	2s
Thomas Lowe, very ill.	2s
Houghton, widow, for child's funeral.	10s
Paid Wm Welch with an apprentice.	£2
Victuals and ale for Days wifes funeral.	4s
Wm Plamers wife for child's bed linen.	6s
A warrant for Thomas Edward.	2s
Pd the constable for serving the same and keeping the man in	

custody all night.	7s
Josiah Pinfield with an apprentice, Charles Allcock's daughter.	£2
Charles Allcocks wife very ill.	2s
Charles Allcocks wife ill.	1s
Charles Allcock.	2s
Pd for examination of Thomas Tidmarsh.	7s

Thomas Tidmarsh was paid 2s himself three days later, so one can only assume his examination proved he was 'settled' in Feckenham. The Charles Allcock entries all took place during the course of one week.

As mentioned before, using the link on The National Archives website will enable you to convert the amounts of money from a certain year into today's equivalent.

Churchwardens' Accounts

A churchwarden's accounts show the financial side of the running of the parish. They list expenditures, such as organ repairs, cleaning, and the buying of bread and wine. They also list the parish rents and rates which were received. For example, the accounts for Feckenham in 1745 show that 'Clarke' was paid £1 5s for winding up the clock and washing the surplus.

The parish official accompanying a removal, or checking on a statement given in an examination and suchlike, could claim back his expenses. An entry in Feckenham for 24 July 1752 states:

For going to Worcester to know if Carpenter of Feckenham had gained a settlement he not paying the levays. 2s 6d.

Often you may see your ancestor's name but it may not say what he is being paid for, but in some cases it does:

1755, Sep 6. Paid Thomas Rowberry for gravel and work done at the church road leading to the school. 10s 8d.

1758, September 20. Pd for a coat for Humphrey Berwick.

There is also a column for credits listing the names of those people who pay rent, and the amount. By 1830 in the Feckenham accounts, details of the properties were also included.

You may see an unusual entry, which regularly appears. The payment for every dead sparrow, or fox, brought to the office, sparrows were then considered vermin, as these examples from 1797 show:

7 February.	Paid for 3 dozen sparrows.	1s 2d
1 April.	Paid for a fox.	1s
14 April.	Paid for a fox.	1s
20 May.	Paid for 4 foxes.	4s
8 July.	Paid for 9 doz young sparrows.	1s 6d
17 July.	2 doz old sparrows.	8d

Other examples through the years include:

8 May 1784.	Paid Wm Boulton for for 3 foxes	3s
2 April 1784.	Paid for a candlestick and sniffers for the vestry	1s. 6d
29 June 1800.	To Jn Baylis for 40 ton of gravel at 1s p. ton.	£2. 0s. 0d
	To 'ditto' for 9½ days work at 2s p.day (in the church yard)	19s
25 January 1807.	Paid organists salary due this day	£6. 5s
30 June 1807.	Paid Mr Richard Wood for repairing and tuning the organ	£3. 3s

Receipts include:

1 December 1805.	Rec'd of Giles Bradley one years rent due Michaelmas last for house and premises belonging to the parish church of Feckenham	£3. 10s
28 April 1805	Rec'd of Mr John Watts one years rent due Lady Day last for church land at Callow Hill	£3. 3s

Poor Law Union and the Workhouse

The Poor Law Amendment Act in 1834 took the decisions away from the parishes and introduced the Poor Law Unions. Parishes were amalgamated together and were formed into a union. Each union had a board of guardians. The unions for Worcestershire were:

Bromsgrove. Alvechurch, Belbroughton, Bentley Pauncefoot, Beoley, Bromsgrove, Clent, Cofton Hackett, Frankley, Grafton Manor, Hagley, Hunnington, Pedmore, Redditch, Romsley, Stoke Prior, Tutnall, Webheath and Wythall.

Droitwich. Claines, Crowle, Crutch, Dodderhill, Doverdale, Droitwich (St Andrew, St Nicholas & St Peter), Elmbridge, Elmley Lovett, Hadzor, Hampton Lovett, Hanbury, Hartlebury, Himbleton, Hindlip, Huddington, Martin Hussingtree, Oddingley, Ombersley, Salwarpe, Stock & Bradley, Tibberton, Upper Mitton, Upton Warren and Warnden.

Dudley. Apart from the parish of Dudley, included parishes in the county of Staffordshire.

Evesham. Abbot's Lench, Aldington, Ashton Underhill, Aston Somerville, Aston sub Edge, Badsey, Bengeworth, Bretforten, Broadway, Childs Wickham, Church Honeybourne, Church Lench, Cleeve Prior, Cow Honeybourne, Evesham (All Saints & St Lawrence), Great & Little Hampton, Harvington, Hinton on the Green, North Littleton, Norton &

Lenchwick, Offenham, Rouse Lench, Sedgeberrow, and South Littleton; and Pebworth, Saintbury, Weston sub Edge, Wickhamford and Willersey in Gloucestershire.

Kidderminster. Bewdley, Chaddesley Corbett, Churchill, Kidderminster, Ribbesford, Rushock, Stone, Stourport with Lower Mitton, Upper Arley and Wolverley.

Kings Norton. Beoley, Kings Norton, and Northfield; Edgbaston in Warwickshire; Harborne in Staffordshire.

Martley. Abberley, Alfrick, Arley Kings, Astley, Bransford, Broadwas, Clifton-upon-Teme, Cotheridge, Doddenham, Great & Little Witley, Grimley, Hallow, Holt, Knightwick, Leigh, Lulsley, Martley, Pensax, Shelsey, Shrawley, Stockton, Suckley and Wichenford.

Pershore. Abberton, Besford, Birlingham, Bishampton, Bredicot, Bricklehampton, Broughton Hackett, Charlton, Churchill, Cropthorne, Defford, Dormston, Eckington, Elmley Castle, Fladbury, Flyford Flavel, Grafton Flyford, Great Comberton, Hill & Moor, Kington, Little Comberton, Naunton Beauchamp, Netherton, North Piddle, Norton-by-Kempsey, Peopleton, Pershore (St Andrew's and Holy Cross), Pinvin, Pirton, Spetchley, Stoulton, Strensham, Throckmorton, Upton Snodsbury, White Ladies Aston, Whittington, Wick and Wyre Piddle.

Shipston-on-Stour. Parishes belonging to Gloucestershire, but also Blockley, Tidmington and Tredington.

Stourbridge. Cakemore, Cradley, Halesowen, Hasbury, Hawn, Hill, Illey, Lapal, Lutley, Lye, Stourbridge, Upper Swinford, Wollaston and Wollescote; and Amblecote, Brierley Hill, Kingswinford and Quarry Bank in Staffordshire.

Tenbury. Berrington, Bockleton, Eastham, Great Kyre, Hanley Child, Hanley William, Knighton upon Teme, Lindridge, Little Kyre, Orleton, Rochford and Tenbury; Boraston, Burford, Greet, Nash and Whitton; Brimfield, Little Hereford and Stoke Bliss in Shropshire and Herefordshire.

Upton-on-Severn. Berrow, Birtsmorton, Bushley, Castle Morton, Croom D'Abitot, Earl's Croome, Eldersfield, Guarlford, Hanley Castle, Hill Croome, Holdfast, Kempsey, Longdon, Madresfield, Malvern, Newland,

Powick, Queenhill, Ripple, Severn Stoke, Upton on Severn and Welland.
Worcester. The parishes within the city.

The board of guardians was elected by those who paid the parish poor rates, and they now controlled the relief paid to the poor. A relieving officer was employed by each union to decide who should qualify for relief. The poor now had to undergo a 'workhouse test'. Those who were able-bodied were forced to go into the workhouse, whereas widows with dependent children, the elderly and the sick could sometimes still be given outside relief. The overseers or churchwardens still collected the poor rate, but now on behalf of the guardians. In 1865 this rate became known as the Union Rate. It was abolished in 1925.

Although workhouses were in existence before 1834 they had been used on a much smaller scale. Now, with the introduction of the new act, they needed to be much larger places. From 1834 each union began to construct larger buildings, the majority of which saw their first 'patients' enter the doors during 1836. The workhouses differed greatly from union to union. Some were actually said to be quite clean and humane; whereas others were as we are shown in books and films today, and to go into one was no different to going to prison.

The introduction of old-age pensions and unemployment benefits in the early 1900s gradually phased out the need for the workhouse, and in 1930 the work of the guardians was transferred to the local authorities. Those who now needed help went before this body of men to whom they could claim benefit for twenty-six weeks. If they still needed help when this period had ended, they then had to take a means test and if it was found that they had anything saleable, they were told to sell it.

When they had passed the means test they would then go weekly to the institute where they waited for their names to be called out. In some cases they were given no particular time at which to attend, so had to be patient. If they were not there when their name was called out they missed their slot and received no benefit. On alternate weeks they were either given their rent or a grocery ticket. They had no choice as to what items they could buy with their ticket; it had been scored off as to what they were entitled to. They also had to tell the officials which shop they were going to use so checks could be made to ensure the grocer only gave them what they were supposed to have, which was very mundane, basic foodstuffs.

All over Worcestershire there is evidence of the old workhouse buildings. Many were turned into hospitals and are still being used today. The Kings Norton workhouse in Raddlebarn Lane was until recently Selly Oak, one of the area's main hospitals, and well-known as the centre of treatment for service personnel injured in Afghanistan. The workhouse at Kidderminster became the Kidderminster General Hospital which has now been extended and modernised so is hardly recognisable as an old workhouse. Some became factories and others have eventually been demolished to make way for housing estates.

The local authorities each inherited their workhouse records but, unfortunately, a lot were made into pulp during the Second World War. However, there are a few which have found their way into county archives. These are mainly the minutes of the regular meetings between the governors and the union officials. It is very rare that you will find any admission books so you may not be able to find when, or if, your ancestors spent any time in the workhouse, unless they were there at the time of a census. In a lot of cases, only initials are listed on the census page.

The majority of records which do exist for Worcestershire are held at the record office at County Hall, Spetchley, but a couple can be found in record offices closer to their location. The records for Dudley workhouse are held at the Dudley Archives and Local History Office in Coseley, and Shipston on Stour's records are in Warwick County Record Office. Stourbridge's workhouse records are in Stafford Record Office, and Kings Norton's in the Birmingham Archives at Birmingham Library.

Again, a search in the Bulk Accessions (BAs) card indexes will give you an indication of what is available. As with the older poor law records, a search under the relevant town for 'poor' or 'guardians of the poor' will point you in the right direction. A general search in the card indexes for 'guardians', 'poor law union' or 'workhouse' will also list what is available. You will then find that each BA number is split into what is called bundles, so you will then have to decide which bundle you want. For example the reference for BA10874 states:

> 220 general ledgers, rate books, valuation lists and other financial records of the former Redditch Urban District Council, Feckenham Rural Council and Redditch Local Board and Alcester and Bromsgrove Poor Law Unions. 1843–1963.

BA10874 then goes on to list the 193 bundles it comprises of, with a brief description of what is in each bundle.

Searching under the word 'Guardians' lists all the unions in name order and takes in the BA numbers 400–414. For example BA401 comprises of 106 bundles from the Droitwich Board of Guardians Archives dating from 1836 to 1927. They include minute books, general ledgers and parochial ledgers. BA402 is the reference for the Evesham Board of Guardians Archives, 1836–1930, and includes registers of births and deaths. BA409 contains the Pershore Board of Guardians Archives that is arranged into sixty-three bundles. One of which includes a minute book from 1835–1925.

A Workhouse Punishment Book for Upton-on-Severn shows the name, the offence, and the punishment inflicted. Such offences included 'making a disturbance', 'abusive language', 'quarrelling' and 'quitting the workhouse without leave'. In most cases the punishment was 'reprimanded by the Board'. However some cases ended in the magistrates' court. Joseph Creese was found 'stealing money from an inmate that died', and Edward King 'receiving some of that money'. They were both 'ordered to be taken before the magistrates' and were there sentenced to fourteen days' imprisonment.

In 1894, one young boy caused the master to make quite a large entry in the book regarding his behaviour and dissapearance two days later:

> September 15. John Lyons, a vagrant lad, admitted three weeks ago by order of the Malvern magistrates and very troublesome. Allowed out to football with other boys, he brought in a small green rod and was threatening to strike another lad with it. Master seeing this at once took

the rod from him and on his being impudent and threatening to kick the Master's legs, he at once put the same rod about his back.

John Lyons absconded in the workhouse clothes on Monday morning September 17. Instead of taking the lad with him to school with the rest of the children as usual porter left the lad behind because his school cap could not be found. Returning the porter did not look him up or report to the master. But the school master reported the boy being absent.

A workhouse parochial ledger is the set of half-yearly accounts between the workhouse and each parish within the union. It can be helpful in that it lists all the parishes within that union, and shows how the size of the parish regulated the amount of county rate. In the Kidderminster parochial ledger for 1868 the payment for Chaddesley Corbett was £128 whereas for Broom it was £24.

The minute books give you an idea of the day-to-day running of the workhouse and you may find an ancestor mentioned there. These examples come from the Kidderminster meeting minutes book for 3 August 1869. After the minutes had been read from the last meeting – and the clerk had reported that he had checked the accounts and invoices and that everything was in order – the meeting, which included twelve men, began. The master asked for disbursements for certain costs; these included 'the funeral costs of Mary Jones'. Various people had come forward since the last meeting offering children in the workhouse a home. Some were perhaps looking for cheap labour, such as Herbert Smith of George Street, Kidderminster, who wanted a servant. Sarah Pitt aged 13 was sent on a month's trial. Others were genuine family members like John Adams of Worcester Street, a carpet weaver; Charlotte Cooper aged 12, an orphan, was his niece and he was offering her a home. She was sent with two lots of clothing.

Another was:

Elizabeth Bennett wife of John Bennett, tinner in the employ of Messrs Baldwin Stourport, living in the parish of Hartlebury applied to the guardians to take Paul Horton, 12 years old, their nephew from the workhouse and to adopt him as their own child.

Resolve that the guardians consent to the boy Horton leaving the workhouse to live with his uncle Bennett and that the boy be supplied with two suits of clothing.

Incidentally, Messrs Baldwin of Stourport was the father of our future Prime Minister, Stanley Baldwin, as already mentioned. Other relations, however, were not so forthcoming:

A letter was produced by the clerk from Samuel Willey Smethwick in reply to one from the clerk that he Willey could not afford to contribute towards his father's support. Mr Wallis, relieving officer, was instructed to make inquiries as to Willey's ability and if he found his means sufficient the clerk was to take steps to summon him before the trustees.

Someone else who seemed to think that he could turn his back on his family once they were in the workhouse was William Inell:

The clerk reported that William Inell had been warned for deserting his children now in the workhouse and that Inell should pay the cost of back maintenance and take the children from the workhouse. A letter was now read from Inell asking that the children be supplied with clothes to which the board declined to accede and the clerk was directed to at once communicate to Inell that if he did not immediately take the children from the workhouse proceedings would be again taken against him.

A list of those receiving outdoor relief was included. Among the ailments listed were 'abscess on leg, bronchitis, rheumatic fever, small pox, bad foot' and 'weak after confinement'.

These books are very large, but if you had an ancestor in the workhouse and they are mentioned in the minutes, it is well worth the search. Two good sites on the Internet for information and history on the workhouse are www.workhouses.org.uk and www.institutions.org.uk.

Non-Conformists

After 1837 finding a non-conformist ancestor is no problem. They were obliged to register their events in the same way as everyone else, so you will find births, marriages and deaths in the same way as any of your other ancestors. From 1841 of course, you will find them in the census. Before 1837, finding their records may be more difficult – apart from marriages, which after 1754 had to take place in the Anglican Church (although there still may be one or two who did not comply with this law).

The majority of non-conformist groups did keep registers but, unfortunately, not all have survived, and not all are available to the general public. Worcester Family History Centre has various registers available on microfilm and a comprehensive index is available to ascertain what is available.

Catholics

Catholic services were held in secret and, in most cases, registers were not kept in order to preserve the anonymity of those participating. However, the parish church generally being the only burial ground available, Catholics had no choice but to bury their dead there. Secret funeral services were often held in the middle of the night.

With no permanent buildings to preach in, catholic priests roamed the country, covering many miles to visit makeshift chapels. Some did keep registers in their bags and those that have survived demonstrate the distances some of these priests travelled. They would stay with Catholic families, often in large houses that accommodated 'priest holes'.

The Catholic Relief Acts of 1778 and 1791 gave Catholics the right to their own places of worship, and it is around this time that registers for Catholics start to become available. There are nine microfilms in Worcester Family History Centre which contain a few Catholic registers for the 1800s and 1900s. However, a more extensive list is held at St Chad's Cathedral in Birmingham. The Archdiocesan Archive Office attached to the cathedral on St Chad's Queensway holds all the registers available for the Midland District, which includes Worcestershire. Also included are the counties of Warwickshire, Staffordshire and Oxfordshire. A booking is necessary to visit the archives and information is available at www.birminghamdiocese.org.uk.

Baptists

Those belonging to the Baptist faith were not baptised until they were adults, but registers were kept for the births that took place among their congregations. However, there was not a set age for baptism so, unlike in the Anglican Church when you can assume a child was less than a year old when baptised, you can never be absolutely sure of the subject's age. There are nine microfilms in Worcester Family History Centre for a few of the churches in Worcestershire. These go from the 1770s to the late 1800s.

Methodists

In 1740 John Wesley introduced the Methodist movement and local societies would hold meetings in its members' houses. Gradually, as the movement spread over England, preaching houses and chapels were erected. In the eighteenth and ninteenth centuries the movement split into different groups: the New Connexion, the Countess of Huntingdon's, the Wesleyan Methodists, the Primitive Methodists, and the United Methodist Church.

The Methodist society was grouped into circuits, each circuit having its own minister who travelled around preaching to each individual congregation. Early records were kept by these preachers, but not many of these registers have survived. There are intermittent registers for numerous chapels available at Worcester Family History Centre on twelve microfilms for the 1800s and 1900s.

Presbyterians

The Presbyterian Church was the established Church of Scotland from the early 1600s and gradually spread south across England. During the Commonwealth (1649–1660) it was the main religious denomination of England. Although Presbyterians were ejected from their parishes following the Restoration, the Act of Toleration in 1689 allowed them to build their own meeting houses. To avoid confusion with the Scottish Presbyterians they called themselves Unitarians.

Most of their registers have survived but as they were kept by a central office they have now been lodged with either the National Archives at Kew, or the United Reformed Church Historical Society at Dr William's Library, Gordon Square, London. There are a few that are still with the local Presbyterian churches themselves. However, there are eight microfilms in Worcester Family History Centre which contain a few registers from the late 1700s to the 1800s.

Other Non-Conformists

Other non-conformists you may come across include the Quakers, the Salvation Army, Huguenots and Jews. There are no registers available in Worcester Family History Centre for these religions. Many non-conformist religions were required to surrender their pre-1837 records to the General Register Office and these are now kept at the National Archives under various classes (reference numbers). Quaker registers can be found under RG6. There is a subscription site where these registers have been digitalised at www.bmdregisters.co.uk. There are also various deeds, minutes of meetings and accounts for the Worcestershire Quakers during the 1800s and 1900s amongst the Bulk Accessions in Worcester Record Office.

The Salvation Army movement grew out of the Methodist Circuit (its founder, William Booth, was originally a Methodist preacher). Although there may be family records kept with the individual branch offices, the majority were kept centrally at the international and national headquarters in London. Unfortunately, this building in Queen Victoria Street was hit during the bombings of the Second World War and many of the registers were destroyed. Contacting the head office will point you in the right direction for any available records.

The Huguenots were Protestants who fled to England, mainly from France, during the sixteenth and seventeenth centuries. Records are held at the National Archives under various classes and the Huguenot Library holds indexes for these references. Their website is www.huguenotsociety.org.uk.

When tracing Jewish ancestors a good source of information is the announcement section of the *Jewish Chronicle*. Copies of this newspaper can be found at the Colindale Newspaper Library. For any family history research the suggested first point of contact is the local synagogue.

Other Records of Use to the Family Historian

There are a great many documents, records and books which can give you information to add depth to your family history beyond the simple events of life and death. They can take you right into the times of the day, to experience the lives your ancestors led and events with which they may have been concerned.

Newspapers

Newspapers are not just useful for the information they can provide on births, marriages and deaths; they can also make fascinating contextual reading. But be warned, you can often get sidetracked when looking for something in an old newspaper. Sometimes you can spot something that has nothing to do with your family but is very interesting all the same!

So what can you find in the newspapers of your ancestor's day? You may find an obituary, or if he was involved in some misdemeanour he may appear in the columns dealing with the quarter sessions or assizes. For those with richer ancestors or ancestors with their own business, you may find they were unfortunate to have become bankrupt and so find their names in the bankruptcy lists. If they suffered a sudden or untoward death the details of their inquest may appear. You may think that as your ancestors were illiterate, they would not have been interested in the newspapers, but this was not always the case. Readings of the local weekly newspaper were often held in the back room of a local public house for anyone who wanted to attend.

When you look at old newspapers you will see that the adverts are more like small reports than just an 'ad'. As in 1786 with Oriental Vegetable Cordial:

For disorders of the stomach and bowels. The extraordinary influence that the Oriental Vegetable Cordial imparts to the stomach from its tonic and invigorating quantities is strongly exemplified by the immediate effects produced in taking it when the stomach is overloaded with food or debilitated by intemperance. To continually weak stomachs it affords a pleasing sensation, it accelerates the proceeds of digestion, corrects crudities and removes the chronic and flactuancies. It diffuses a genial warmth that cherishes the animal spirits and takes away the listlessness and languor that so greatly embitters the hours of nervous people.

In 1861 you could read about Christian's Dandelion Chocolate:

This new and most agreeable diet for breakfast, luncheon or supper is invaluable to persons who may be predisposed to afflictions of the liver, spasms, flatuency, weak digestion or general debility. As a regular breakfast beverage its use will prevent bilious attacks and keep the liver in a healthy condition. A cupful may be prepared without the slightest trouble and ready for use in less than three minutes. Sold in packets, 6d, 1s and 2s each.

Looking at the *Berrow's Worcester Journal* in 1832, the front page is covered with small reports extolling the virtues of some product you ancestor may have been using themselves:

Macassar Oil patronised and sanctioned by their gracious majesties and their Royal Highnesses the Duchess of Kent and the Princess Victoria.
    The merits of Macassar Oil in rendering the human hair soft, glossy and consequently beautiful are well known. Imported from the Island of Macassar situated near Borneo in the East Indies by Kendall and Son

they feel the greatest of pleasure in being able to announce that they will henceforth vend an oil for one shilling and six pence.

Sold at the Civet Cat, 18 Foregate Street, Worcester.

All these sorts of adverts help us imagine what our ancestors may have been buying. But there are other things in newspapers to interest us.

You will see properties for sale by auction or to be let, and mistresses who are advertising their schools. There is a public announcements section, the births, marriages and deaths – although in those times only the upper classes would advertise their events.

While reading through the newspapers you may come across something quite by accident relating to your family. Say your ancestor was related to a Thomas Griffiths, or even a William Smith, a piece like this from July 1794 would add a little more history to the family:

Two Guineas Reward – Whoever will apprehend William Smith late of the Toll Gatherers at Worcester Bridge, charged by the Coroner's Inquest with Manslaughter, so that he be brought before a magistrate for the City of Worcester shall immediately receive the above reward of 2 guineas from Ann Griffin of Leigh Sinton in the County of Worcester, the widow of Thomas Griffiths, lately deceased. The said William Smith is a thin raw-boned man, remarkably upright about five feet eight inches high of a pale sallow complexion, long visage, very dark brown hair nearly approaching black, sometimes tied and at other times in rollers: his eyes of dark hazel. He is suspected to be 28 years of age and is a native of Worcester vicinity. He is by trade a cordwainer and had on when he went from Worcester, on 28th April last, either a blue livery great coat with yellow buttons and stand up collar or else a servants jacket and waistcoat made of light grey Bath coating with yellow buttons and leather breeches.

Wealthier members of society may have attended balls and soirees which were reported by the local newspapers. There were no photographs to show us what they may have been wearing but the reports contained graphic descriptions. Such as this report from the *Aris Gazette* in June 1800:

To enumerate the different dresses our limits forbid us. It must suffice for us to remark that the prevailing colours were lilac, yellow and green. Chamberry muslins were much worn; also coloured crepe and flowers. The hair was dressed in the Grecian style, without powder, to show the back of the neck, in bows, flattened with combs of diamond, gold etc. The front of the neck rather more covered than has lately been the fashion; ear-rings chiefly drop diamonds. Scarcely a lady appeared without a wreath of diamonds or pearls, some capes richly spangled and trimmed with silver. Vandykes were worn. Several Paradise plumes also appeared. Bandeaus were much worn, and a profusion of feathers, diamonds, topazes and antiques were general. The gentlemen wore buff coloured silk stockings and the steel and pearl manufacturers were much encouraged, as appeared from the number of sets of steel, and steel set in pearl, buttons on the coats, steel hoops in the hats, sword knots etc.

And in January 1851:

Magnificent stamped material of sky blue with embroidered bouquets in white and silver, the bottom of the front breadth was embroidered (in the form of an apron) with large flowers, fastened with light hanging foliage and large bows, the skirt was raised over a white satin under-skirt by two bouquets composed of leaves of blue velvet and some small feathers mixed with silver cords; the same kind of bouquets were plaited in the hair, over which was worn a very light silver net-work. The body of this Pompadour robe was trimmed with a new and beautiful fringe of white and blue feathers which harmonises well with the white shoulders it encircles.

Another was a magnificent apricot coloured taffeta, trimmed with three deep flounces round which was a broad wreath of flowers embroidered in silk of the natural colours producing a fresh and lively appearance. The body embroidered to match. The same kind of dress in colours is seen in white taffetas, which is much younger and not less elegant.

As has already been mentioned, there are no coroner's reports available for Worcestershire so it is necessary to search the local newspapers. The

Bromsgrove, Droitwich and Redditch Weekly Messenger for Saturday 19 July 1873, gives a sad story which brings up all sorts of questions when searching for our ancestors and certainly shows us that things may not always be straightforward:

FECKENHAM. An inquest was held on Thursday at the Lygon Arms before W S P Hughes. Esq., coroner for the district on the body of Jane Cull, wife of Joseph Edward Cull, veterinary surgeon, of Inkberrow. Mr Stacey was foreman of the jury.

Jane Kings, married woman, deposed: I am not in the habit of acting as midwife, but I agreed with Eliza Baylis, about five weeks ago, to attend deceased, who was living with W Hill, labourer, as man and wife. I know by reports deceased has had several children by Hill. I was called by him at three or four on Wednesday morning. I found her very ill, and in about half an hour the child was born. I have had thirteen children, but never acted as midwife before. I applied cold water to her face, and gave her a cup of tea nearly cold. Deceased grew faint and I began to be afraid. She would not let me send for a doctor because she was afraid of being sent to the workhouse, and her husband would have to pay the money back. I had fears about her, but could not go for the doctor. Hill was downstairs. Deceased died about seven o'clock. Eliza Baylis came just before she died. I had sent for her three times because I did not like to be alone with deceased. I suggested we should send for Dr Leacroft. He came directly, but deceased had been dead ten minutes. She asked me to get her a crust of bread before she died. I did so, and she ate part of it. There was no oatmeal or anything in the house. Accordingly to my idea she died in a faint. The child was born alive and healthy.

In answer to the foreman witness said she sent for Eliza Baylis because she had been engaged by her. Though she had sent three times, first at four o'clock, she did not come until seven o'clock alleging she could not get up in the morning. The Foreman: Why not have you sent for the doctor? If you could send for Baylis by Hill you could have sent for the doctor.

The coroner severely censured the witness for undertaking duties she was utterly unqualified for, and for not having sent for Dr Leacroft.

Dr Leacroft deposed: I was sent for about seven o'clock and got up immediately, but while I was dressing Hill called and said the woman was dead. I have known the woman about twenty years, and have attended her in her confinements whilst she was living with her husband, but not since. She had been living with Hill and other men. I saw her about a month since. She asked me if I would attend her, and promised to pay me, but I know from their way of living and utter destitution she could not possibly do so. I told her in answer to her question as to getting a note from the relieving officer, that he would have to ask the consent of the Guardians, who, knowing how she was living with Hill, might perhaps refuse. She told me she had engaged Eliza Baylis to be with her, and I told her she was quite incompetent, and advised her to go to the workhouse until she was well, and then leave the man Hill. I told her that if am emergency should arise she could get a note from an overseer who lives in the village. I found her on her back dead. She was pale, as though she had died from syncope caused by loss of blood. She had the appearance of being ill-nourished, and there was such a want of tone about her system, that even if I had been in attendance, probably the woman might have died. Proper attention had been paid to the child.

W. Hill deposed: I am a labourer, and have lived with the deceased knowing she was the wife of a married man. I knew it was very wicked. I went for the doctor when I was ordered. I did all I could.

The coroner, in addressing the jury, said it was a sad case of the result of immorality, but no criminal guilt seemed to rest on any one.

Verdict: Death from syncope in childbirth, caused by want of proper attention.

The coroner severely censured Hill, and begged him to live a different life.

The burials register for Feckenham shows that Jane Cull, aged 38, was buried on 19 July 1873. Frederick Cull, son of Jane Cull of Feckenham, was baptised on 22 February 1874.

On the 1871 census for Alcester Road, Feckenham, Jane Cull and her children, Albert, Edith and Arthur, are living next door to William Hill who is eleven years Jane's junior, and in 1881, Frederick is living with Joseph Cull's parents, as their grandson. Anyone descended from Frederick would believe Joseph to be his father; they may wonder why Joseph's name does not appear on the baptism register. But if they obtained Jane's death certificate, which would show that there was an inquest into her death, and then looked for a report into her inquest in the paper, they would then know the sad truth.

Worcester Family History Centre holds all the newspapers for Worcester, as well as those for certain Worcestershire towns such as Kidderminster, Evesham and Bromsgrove. However local Worcestershire libraries hold the old newspapers for their area. The newspaper library at Collindale in London holds papers for the whole country.

The Times Digital Archive can make an interesting search even if you think your ancestor may not have achieved sufficient notoriety to appear in this newspaper. It can be found online at www.worcestershire.whub.org.uk. Click on 'Libraries and Learning', then 'Computers and 24 Hour Services', and then 'Online Reference Books and Newspapers', and finally 'Infotrack Custom Newspapers'. You do need a Worcestershire library barcode, which appears on a local library ticket. If looking at other library sites, *The Times* Digital Archive can be accessed through all county library websites using a local library's membership ticket for that particular county. Many libraries and record offices have access to *The Times* Digital Archive on their public computers. The years covered are 1785–1985. If you type 'Worcestershire' into the search tab, over 40,000 hits will be returned. These hits are split up into different categories.

'Advertising' will bring up particulars of sales or auctions on properties all over Worcestershire. Also included will be the classified advertisements. 'Editorial and Commentary' will list all the articles concerning general news items within Worcestershire. Whereas 'News' gives you reports of the Worcester assizes, parliamentary news and visits made by the royal family to other notable families in Worcestershire. 'Business' details the state of trade, trade union meetings and strikes – articles relating to the building of the railways can also be found here. 'Features' includes the weather, sport events and the theatre. In the 'People' category you'll find obituaries, official appointments and bankruptcy details. You can also search for a specific town, surname or event.

Another useful newspaper is the *London Gazette*. This has its own website: www.london-gazette.co.uk. You need to search in the 'search archive' tab, and again typing the word 'Worcestershire' brings up numerous results. Asking for the 'oldest first' in the 'sort by date' tab takes you right back into the late seventeenth century.

Cemeteries and Monumental Inscriptions

At the start of the nineteenth century the population, particularly in the larger industrial towns, was beginning to increase. This was reflected in the parish churchyard, which was becoming increasingly over-crowded with graves. In some places numerous burials took place in one plot, the last burial being perhaps just 2ft below ground. It was soon realised that this situation was making churchyards extremely unsanitary places.

During the cholera epidemic of 1831–32 tens of thousands died, and it became apparent that something should be done regarding the burial of the dead. Private companies began developing burial grounds but a second cholera epidemic in 1848 forced the government to intervene. The burial acts, which took place during the years 1852–57, eventually put in place the system we know today. Burial boards were created within the town councils and they were made responsible for the burial of the dead. Using money from the borough rates the board began building cemeteries and arranging the fees, charges, and the sale of certain burial plots. The cemeteries were divided into sections; some ground was consecrated for the burial of Anglicans and other sections were un-consecrated for the burial of non-conformists. Still other sections were kept specifically for public burial – for those who could not afford to purchase their own plots. When searching the registers you may find your ancestor buried with a complete stranger.

There is a good collection of records for most of the cemeteries in Worcestershire at Worcester Family History Centre, as follows:

Bromsgrove	1858–1994
Hagley	1908–1994
Kidderminster	1878–1993
Pershore	1894–1978
Redditch	1855–1950
Stourbridge	1879–1910
Upton on Severn	1866–1996
Worcester, Astwood	1858–1989
Worcester, St John	1893–1989
Worcester, Tallow Hill	1823–1895

There are different types of cemetary records available. The burial register is similar to the normal parish burial registers except that it will also give the date of death, and details of the grave (i.e. the section and the grave number). When you have found the section and grave number you can then

Ivy and other plants often grow over monuments making them difficult, sometimes impossible, to read.

consult the grave register which will show you who else is buried in that grave, when they were buried, and their age. If it is a purchased grave this register will also tell you who originally purchased the plot.

The Monumental Inscriptions Indexes (MIs) is an ongoing project being undertaken by local family history societies, however there is already a large collection of MIs, and many volumes for the churchyards of Worcestershire are held at Worcester Family History Centre. Once again, remember these transcripts, although undertaken by experienced family historians, can still be flawed by human error. Many old gravestones are difficult to read due to erosion; it is sometimes hard to define a small number or letter obliterated or obscured by moss, ivy and erosion. Time and neglect has caused many gravestones to become only ruins, some of which have been removed by the appropriate officials. Of course, many of our ancestors would not have been able to afford an expensive monument. But for those who could, many erected large edifices in tribute to their deceased loved-ones and composed long verses to commemorate their life as these examples from Wribbenhall and Catshill show:

There is sweet rest in Heaven
In loving remembrance of
Elizabeth
Wife of David Lowe
Of Habberley Road, near Bewdley
Who died March 13, 1875
Aged 63 years
Then let us fly, to Jesus fly,
Whose powerful arm can save
Then shall our hopes ascend on high
And triumph o'er the grave
And also of the above named
David Lowe
Who sweetly fell asleep
April 2, 1894
Aged 80 years

I've reached at length my native land
The place I truly love; Glad in my Saviours spotless robe
I've joined the hosts above
In loving Memory of
Mary Lowe
Who passed away March 17, 1909
Aged 63 years
Peace, perfect peace, with loved ones far away
In Jesus meeting we are safe.

In Memory of
Samuel Rooke
Born August 8th, 1811
Died January 3rd, 1886
And hast thou gone! Forever gone
And left us here to weep
Till we are called to follow thee
And in the grave to sleep
But since thou could'st no longer stay
To cheer us with thy love
We hope to meet with thee again
In yon bright home above.

Wills

Worcestershire wills held at Worcester Family History Centre go back as far as the fifteenth century and cover nearly 500 years, the last year available being 1928. All the wills are indexed but it is only the volume 1858–1928 which gives a page number for the appropriate year; the indexes between 1660 and 1857 just give the date. So when searching the microfilm for that period you will need to go to the start of the appropriate month of the year and search right through that month as the wills are not in chorological order either. The earlier indexes give a number for the will.

A typical will gives the deceased's address and occupation. It could be only one page long stating: 'I give and bequeath all the residue of my real and personal estate unto...' Or it could be twelve pages long, or more; naming individual children and their individual bequests, other members of the family, a servant being given just a small amount of money in recognition of their service, or perhaps a piece of jewellery or furniture. If property was owned from which rent was received, each address could be named and to which son or daughter it was being left. Be prepared to read through a lot of legal jargon.

This example is taken from the will of Charles Keyte of Blockley, dated 3 May 1911:

> To my son Albert William Keyte absolutely my Bureau and my picture of Torquay. To my son Harry Keyte absolutely my two pictures of Saint Peter and Saint John. To my son Frank Keyte absolutely my silver watch chain and small organ. To my son Charles Keyte absolutely my gold watch chain and silver watch and also my tools and effects of every kind belonging to me in connection with my trade of a carpenter and wheelwright and the stock of timber and other stock in trade thereto belonging and the Goodwill of my said business. I give and bequeath to my said wife Jane Keyte absolutely all my wines liquors provisions and consumable stores and also such articles of my furniture or other effects of domestic or household use or ornament.

In earlier wills it was usual for a husband to make provisions for his property and monies after his wife's death, therefore making it unnecessary for her to make her own will.

Many early wills may contain an inventory. It was law until 1782 – after which it was the personal decision of one of the interested parties. This would be included with the will, listing all the deceased's belonging, as this example from 1745 shows:

> Goods and chattels of William Price late of the parish of St Peter's Droitwich in the County of Worcestershire Husbandman Deceased dated 13 June 1745:

Wearing apparel and money	£1. 10s. 0d
In kitchen, all things priced at	£1. 0s. 0d
Parlour: bed and other things	£3. 0s. 0d
3rd room: bed and other goods	£2. 0s. 0d
The things in the day house priced at	£0. 15s. 0d
In the Buttery – 5 barrels	£0. 15s. 0d
The beds and other things in ye two chambers	£1. 15s. 0d
The wheat store growing	£10. 0s. 0d
The barley	£2. 10s. 0d
Twelve acres of grass and clover	£8. 0s. 0d
Four cows	£10. 0s. 0d
One gilding, two mares and colts	£10. 0s. 0d
One yearling colt	£2. 2s. 0d
Twelve ewes and lambs	£3. 0s. 0d
One sow and eight pigs	£2. 0s. 0d
One wagon and two tumbrels	£10. 0s. 0d
Two ploughs and harrow	£0. 15s. 0d
In the barn and farm	£0. 5s. 0d
Geese and poultry	£0. 10s. 0d
The horse gears	£1. 5s. 0d
Things forgotten and not apprised	£0. 5s. 0d

Signed by Joseph Chance and John Langford

Wills and admons belonging to the Peculiar Jurisdiction have also been indexed and filmed, and are kept in the drawers with the other probate and administrations.

A line from the will of William Lucas of Redditch, dated 16 August 1782, should also be mentioned: 'I give and bequeath to my daughter-in-law Catherine James the sum of one hundred pounds to be paid to her upon the attainment of her age of twenty one years or the day of marriage which shall first happen after my decease.' In those times 'daughter-in-law' was the term used to also refer to a step-daughter. In most cases it can be deduced as to the relationship between the two people, but sometimes a little further research may be needed. It would seem in this case Catherine, being under twenty-one and unmarried, is William's step-daughter.

The Principle Probate Registry was introduced in January 1858 following the Court of Probate Act in 1857. This established a Principle Court and forty other district courts across the country. The National Probate Calendar Index lists every will proved in the country alphabetically, by surname. These indexes are available in Worcester Family History Centre and go up to 1943. If a probate is found you can apply to the Probate Registry in York for an office copy of this will.

Directories

The *Kelly's Directory* or Post Office directories of the nineteenth century will give you all sorts of information regarding the county and the towns, small or large, within the county. They do not list everybody in that town like the census does, but if your ancestor had a business or trade you will be able to follow their career through from its beginnings up to their retirement or when they died; the different addresses they may have worked from; and when any of their children may have joined them.

A typical *Kelly's Directory* for Worcestershire will give a brief description of the county as it was at that time. It will list the registration districts in operation for a particular year; the different unions and the parishes which belonged to them; and the 'hundreds' and the parishes which belonged to them. It also lists important buildings such as prisons, hospitals, polling places, the names of the members of parliament for the county, and the police stations.

Each town is then listed alphabetically. A brief narrative is given of important features in that parish, and a description of the church and its history. Then a list of the trades of people working and residing in that town – but bear in mind they had to pay for inclusion so may not necessarily be there. Hamlets are listed under the parish to which they belong.

At the back of most volumes you will find a trades directory. Here trades are listed alphabetically and tradesmen from the whole county, with their addresses, are listed together. You will find anything from accountants to bricklayers, dairymen to farmers, iron founders to leather dressers, shopkeepers to wheelwrights. There is even a list of all public houses in Worcestershire and their licensees. In some directories you will find elaborate adverts. These examples are from an 1884 *Kelly's Directory*:

MALVEN HOUSE BOARDING ESTABLISHMENT
Great Malvern
Joseph Matthews, Proprietor
This house is magnificently and centrally situated, and commands extensive views of the Malvern Hills and surrounding country. It is within ten minutes walk of the Railway Station; contiguous to the Priory Church, Post Office and the Haywell Baths, the House being supplied with water from this celebrated spring.
The rooms, both public and private, and also well adapted for families, are arranged *'en suite'* so as to avoid the fatigue of stairs
(this being an especial boon to invalids)
In the public room, Breakfast is served at 8.00 am in summer, and 9 am in winter; luncheon at 1, tea in Drawing Room at 4, Table d'hote at 7; tea, coffee or cocoa at 9 pm.

Edward Humphries, engineer, of Atlas Works, Pershore announced that he was the manufacturer of the 'All England Prize' Thrashing Machine. He also manufactured steam engines, boilers, corn grinding mills, sewing machinery and cider making machinery. Illustrated catalogues were written in English, French, German and Russian.

W. Bartlett & Sons of Redditch (est. 1750) were patentees of 'Perfect Eyed Needles'. They manufactured needles, sewing machine needles, fish hooks and fishing tackle 'of every description of the finest and most superior qualities'.

Benjamin Parkes & Sons manufactured 'Fenders, Fire Irons, Ash Pans etc' and also 'Hat and Umbrella Stands' in their premises at Woodsetton Works, Near Dudley. They also had a London office at 122 Newgate Street, EC.

H.D Skidmore at Atlas Tube Works, Netherton, near Dudley was a manufacturer of wrought iron tubes and fitting for gas, steam and water.

Morton Stanley (est.1863) manufactured needles, fish hooks, fishing rods and fishing tackle at his Central Works, Redditch. He was also the 'sole manufacturer of the Registered Baiting Needle'.

The directories are available into the 1900s, and you will find some less detailed directories for the late 1700s.

Electoral Registers

The Representation of the People Act in 1832 completely changed the way Parliament was elected and franchised. Many reforms took place during the 1800s but, importantly, this act introduced the electoral register as a way to keep lists of all those entitled to vote. It did not give votes to the working class, but it did take away the power the landed gentry had had since 1688 and give a large portion to the middle class.

In 1832 only male owners of property worth at least £10 were eligible to vote. This ruling changed in 1867 to owners of property worth at least £5, or those who occupied land and paid annual rent of £50 or more. In 1884 all owners of dwelling houses and occupiers who paid rent of £10 were included. Following the First World War, all men over 21 and women over 30 who were householders or wife of householder, were also eligible. In 1928 all women over 21 were included – which meant that all persons over the age of 21 could vote. So the electoral registers from 1918 will list almost every address in the county.

The early electoral registers are in name order and are handwritten. The county is divided up into two divisions – the Eastern Division and the Western Division – and then the two divisions are spit into polling districts. Each district then includes each parish alphabetically (although on some, the filming of these registers seems to have upset the alphabetical format for some reason). The lists give the person's name, place of abode, nature of qualification and the qualifying address – which can be different to the place of abode. The 'nature of qualification' can give various descriptions; 'freehold house and land', 'copyhold estate £100 per year rent' or 'occupier/tenant of farm £50 per annum'.

This format remained the same (apart from eventually being typed) until 1884 when it was supposed to be changed to list the streets alphabetically, showing the individuals eligible at each address. However on the whole this wasn't adhered to until 1918, and even then some smaller towns and villages kept the name order format, right into the early 1930s.

No registers were taken during the First World War. In 1918 the list of qualification changed to:

R   Residence qualification
BP   Business premises qualification
O   Occupational qualification
HO   Qualification through husband's occupation
NM   Naval or military voter

Divisions were now named and also separated into Parliamentary Divisions and Electoral Divisons. For example, Evesham Division, Stourbridge Division, Kidderminster Division. The individual polling districts were also named, so the parish of Upton Warren was in the Electoral Division of Hartlebury, which was in the polling district of Cutnall Green in the Evesham Parliamentary Division.

It sounds complicated but when searching for an individual parish it does help to pinpoint it as you search through the registers. Once you have found your parish in one year, you know exactly where to go for the next year.

The Worcestershire electoral registers are on microfilm and are available for the years 1843–1959.

Land Tax Assessments

This tax was introduced in 1692 as a means of collecting revenue and remained in operation until 1963. The assessments were administered locally and the survival of land tax records fares much the same as many other records and varies from county to county. Those for Worcestershire are available on microfilm from 1780 to 1832. This coincides with the period of time when duplicates were made. After 1832 and the passing of the Representation of the People Act – which introduced the electoral register – duplication was no longer needed. The assessments were then lodged with the Clerk of the Peace and used to establish voting qualification. The single copies of the Land Tax Assessments were once more liable to be lost, although they can often be found amongst the Quarter Session papers.

The records are divided into each 'hundred' and then alphabetically into each separate parish. There are four columns listing the name of the proprietor, the name of the occupier, the sum assessed and the sum exonerated. From this information you will get an idea of who owned property in the parish, how much property they owned and who rented the property from them. It is also a good way of ascertaining who was in the parish at a particular time. However, as the land and property is not named, you won't find out where your ancestor lived, and it should be noted that owners may have had properties in other places so a thorough search needs to be undertaken. Don't forget: if your ancestor was a mere labourer you will probably not find his name in these records.

The tax was levied on land valued at more than 20s and the charge was a fixed sum determined by the government. From 1798 an owner could pay a fifteen-year lump sum and a third of land-owners took up this option. Because of this, some won't appear on the annual returns.

Hearth Tax Returns

Another tax introduced to raise additional revenue was the Hearth Tax, in operation between 1662 and 1689. This tax was levied on those whose house was estimated at being worth 20s or more per annum and those who already paid church or poor rates. They paid 2s per year for each fire hearth in their house. Those not eligible to be taxed had to provide an exemption certificate which had been signed by the vicar, the churchwardens and the overseers of the poor.

The parish constable was responsible for both the issuing of the papers , which were then sent to the clerk of the Justices of the Peace, and for the collection of the taxes half-yearly at Michaelmas and on Lady Day.

Houses from this period are noticeable for their numerous chimneys as it was a way for the rich to build their homes as a show of their wealth.

The returns are on microfilm at Worcester Family History Centre; an example of a typical exemption certificate reads:

These are to certifie whom it shall or may concern that John Grasier of Bishampton in the countie of Worcester hath a cottage house in Bishampton aforesayd not worth above twenty shillings per annual and we doe conceive (according to the Act) that he is not chargeable for his hearth; And moreover he is a very poor man having a wife and a great charge of children to maintaine by his hard labour and very like to fall upon the parish charge. Given under our hands this 7th day of March 1662. Ffrancis Reynolds Vicar of Bishampton.

The lists of those who paid are split in the appropriate 'hundreds', then the individual parish. From the lists for 1663 a fee of 1s was charged for each hearth. It seems that most only had one hearth. For example in Kidderminster there were twenty people with just one hearth, whereas John Allen was the only one with two.

'The Victoria County History of Worcestershire'

The aim of this publication was to tell the story of the county's growth from pre-historic times to the date of its publication in 1906. There are four volumes available, plus an index.

It is a valuable read for any family historian who wants to build a picture of life during a certain period or the place a certain ancestor lived. There are chapters dedicated to the geology of Worcestershire, plus botany, birds, insects and mammals alongside chapters on early man, the Romans and the Domesday Survey. Information about the social and economical history;

the ecclesiastical and political history (with details of all the churches in Worcestershire); the industry, agriculture and sports associated with Worcestershire; and a chapter about certain schools and their histories also feature. There then follows detailed histories of each individual place in Worcestershire. This section is divided into the 'hundreds' and each individual place is found in its respective 'hundred' in alphabetical order. There are also family histories of the important people of the place and details of the people who lived at certain houses in the town.

The books are well illustrated with old photographs and drawings. A website is being produced which holds digital copies of the publication which can be found at www.victoriacountyhistory.ac.uk.

Court Records

Assizes

Worcestershire belonged to the Oxford circuit which also included Gloucestershire, Herefordshire, Shropshire, Staffordshire, Oxfordshire and Berkshire.

The assizes were the principal criminal courts and were presided over by judges visiting from Westminster. These judges would travel over the whole circuit holding courts wherever there was a county gaol. The visits were only held twice a year, in February or March and July or August, so a prisoner could find himself held in the county gaol for a number of months waiting for the next assizes.

Unfortunately there are not many records left detailing the cases that were held at the assizes and the ones that are left are held at the National Archives at Kew. They can be found under Class ASSI. But searching the newspapers will give you reports of any cases your ancestor may have been involved in.

The first pointer you will get when looking through the newspaper is an announcement, a couple of weeks prior to the judges' arrival, that the assizes will be opening on a certain date. For example in 1832 the *Berrow's*

Worcester Journal announced in its edition dated Thursday, 16 February that the hearings would open on Saturday, 3 March.

Then the 1 March edition announced that the circuit had commenced at Reading on the previous Friday. It also added that there were forty-three prisoners awaiting trial in the Worcester county gaol; including Mary Burford, aged 22, for the murder of her bastard child, John Cox, aged 62, for unlawfully abusing Sarah Blakeway; and Jonas Woodall, aged 18, and John Poole, aged 19, who had both been charged with wilfully killing Joseph Holmes. The rest amounted to thirteen prisoners for house-breaking, eleven for sheep-stealing, five for horse-stealing, one for highway robbery, five for poaching and four special jury cases.

The following week there was a full page report on the assizes. The assizes had been opened by Sergeant Pike on the Saturday and then the two judges had arrived on the Sunday. They had dined with the bishop of Worcester then presided over the assizes on the Monday and Tuesday. Considering that one murder case can take weeks to try in this day and age, you will be surprised to read that all the forty-three cases were dealt with in just the two days. They had carried on late into the Tuesday evening which meant that the newspaper, which was published on a Thursday, wrote that 'cases were still proceeding when went to press'. So to read about the final cases you need to go on to the next week's edition.

Searching *The Times* on the Internet can give you reports, albeit in shorter detail, of the assizes for Worcester. Search using the words 'Oxford Circuit' and 'Worcester'.

The assizes on 11 March 1834 were asked to determine the legitimacy of a Mrs C. Anderton. This case went back to 1794 when a John Moore of Dudley married a Miss Holbeche; 'a young lady of great personal attractions.' After two years John Moore discovered his wife was committing adultery with a Mr Corfield. In May 1797 Mrs Moore gave birth to a daughter who was the plaintiff in this case, Mrs Anderton. She wanted to prove that she was the daughter of John Moore and evidence was given that although her mother had moved to London with Mr Corfield, there was a period of five days when she had returned to Worcester and on one particular occasion visited her husband. He was staying at the Crown Inn and it was said 'they were in a parlour alone for some time.' The judge found in favour of Mrs Anderton and decided she was the legitimate daughter of John Moore.

On the night of 18 June 1827 Robert Webb and Thomas Bentam broke into the house of James Beasley, the vicar of Feckenham, and stole various items of silver including a toast rack, vinaigrette and muffineer. Robert Webb was seen acting suspiciously the next day by a ditch and on inspection the toast rack was found wrapped in a handkerchief. His accomplice was chased into a field where he was found to be carrying the vinaigrette and the muffineer. They were both found guilty and sentenced to death.

In 1837 at the assizes on 7 March, Baron Bolland was unable to appear due to injuries reserved in a fire. He was, however, being tried as having started the fire. He had been seen on 11 July the previous year by the granary, cart house and straw house which belonged to Captain Edward Collier. These buildings were on fire but witnesses could not decide whether Bolland was coming away from the buildings, having set fire to them, or going to them, in order to help put the fire out. The judge told the jury there was not enough evidence to convict him and returned a verdict of not guilty.

Quarter Sessions

The quarter sessions were held by the justices of the peace. They dealt with crimes deemed less serious such as theft, poaching, assault, vagrancies and recusants. They also supervised the upkeep of the highways, footpaths and bridges, and local defences, and dealt with tax matters, the taking of oaths and the licensing of trades and alehouses. In some cases they have been known to deal with settlements, removals and bastardy examinations, shops using incorrect weights and measures, or the failure of tradesmen to display their names on their carts.

A look at the subject index in Worcester Family History Centre for 1829–1833 lists others dealt with during those years; the promotion and replacements of local constables, cruelty and injury to animals, embezzlement, false pretences, hawking, idleness, nuisance, rape, riot (including breaking machinery) and trespass. They also acted in cases of illegitimacy. The 1829–1833 index lists numerous cases and includes witness statements stating the child had been born to the mothers. Certain cases heard were sometimes transferred to the assizes due to them 'being of a capital nature'.

As the name suggests the sessions met four times a year – at Easter, Midsummer, Michaelmas and Epiphany (April, July, October and January) – and you will find records for the quarter sessions in the County Record Office at County Hall, Spetchley. You can also search the newspapers for information, as again there were large reports printed on the sessions.

The *Berrow's Worcester Journal* for Thursday, 5 April 1832 published another, almost full page, report of the cases heard that week. They included riot and assault, fraud and a settlement case concerning the family of Thomas Bradley, who had been convicted of theft at the previous assizes, and was now in the county gaol. A removal order to transpose his wife Mary and children Henry, Edmund and Charlotte from the hamlet of Stock and Bradley to Hanbury was issued.

Other examples are from the year before, 3 January 1831:

William Boulton aged 21 for breaking into the house of T Evans of Feckenham, and stealing a crown piece and other money – Seven Years Transportation.

John Flinn pleaded guilty to a charge of stealing two lead weights the property of Jos. Stock of Kings Norton.

Sam. Walters, Wm Forrest and Francis Westwood were charged with stealing 7 geese the property of Samuel Phillips of Northfield. Walters was found guilty and sentenced to fourteen years transportation, it being verified to the Crown that he had been convicted in 1827 and sentenced to twelve months imprisonment. Forrest and Westwood were acquitted.

Thomas Munsloe aged 21 blacksmith was put to the bar charged with breaking a needle machine belonging to Mr Thos Baylis of Tardebigge. The jury having returned a verdict of guilty, the other five men charged with a similar offence, Thos Price, T Mils, J Andrews, Jas Gibbons and T Wilton asked leave to withdraw their plea of not guilty, this being permitted they pleaded guilty. On their return the chairman said that in consequence of their previous good conduct and the humane recommendation of the prosecutor, the Court would pass upon them the lenient sentence of twelve months imprisonment of hard labour.

The normal sentence for this crime would have been seven years' transportation.

The *Berrow's Worcester Journal* for Saturday, 9 January 1858 reported the quarter sessions of the previous week: John Staight, a so-called maltser, was sentenced to nine months' imprisonment for obtaining some sacks of barley from a farmer in Moor, near Fladbury, and then not paying him. The farmer, William Wagstaff, went to look for the malthouse in Worcester but found it did not exist. He later saw John Staight at the railway station who told him he couldn't pay him then, as he had not been paid himself.

On 2 December 1857 it was discovered that lead had been taken from the roof of St Peter's Church in Droitwich. The next day some lead had turned up in Birmingham and Mr Hyatt, the church warden, had gone over there. A patch on pieces of the lead matched where a chimney was positioned, this proved it was the lead from St Peter's. The police waited at the shop where the lead had been taken to and when John Davies returned for his money, he was arrested. However there was no proof that he had stolen the lead; Davies said someone else had given it to him, so the judge agreed that it was a difficult case. He felt there were others involved who should be standing with the prisoner, but he did feel that the prisoner had knowingly taken the lead to Birmingham. The jury found John Davis guilty of receiving stolen goods and he was sentenced to twelve months' hard labour. As he left the court he shouted 'innocent, above suspicion!'

A carpet weaver from Kidderminster, William Stone, was charged with stealing from his employers Messrs William Henry and Joseph Worth. He had been seen taking a bag with him as he left the premises, and when it was searched was found to contain skeins of cotton, a ball of string and other items. When his house was searched similar items were found. William was found guilty but because of his length of service, of about twenty years, and his previous good conduct the judge was lenient with him. He only gave him four months' hard labour.

To look at the original papers for the quarter sessions can be quite time-consuming unless you are looking for a particular case. Each quarter has been separated into bundles which are kept in boxes. You can look at the index and find in which bundle of papers the particular entry is in. However, just by looking through a particular session you can find all sorts of items which weren't reported in the newspaper.

Papers also show accounts for various parish requirements, as this one from 3 January 1831: 'The treasurer of the county of Worcester to James Williams for conveying vagrants from Michaelmas 1830 to Epiphany 1831.' He removed eighty-six in total during that time and charged varying amounts per mile. Sometimes 10d a mile, sometimes 8d and occasionally just 4d a mile.

There were also the treasury reports from the previous quarter which show the receipts from parish officers, the county rates, the county's share of the prisoners' earnings and other expenditures. For example the account from the Michaelmas Sessions, 1829–1830 listed such receipts as:

Amount of cash received for County Rates	£7809. 14s. 2d
Goods sold to various persons from stock of manufactory in the gaol	£46. 0s. 0d
The county's share of the prisoners' earnings in the gaol	£152. 15s. 2½d
Ditto for work done for tradesmen	£75. 8s. 9d

And examples of the expenditures were:

Salary to gaoler	£150. 0s. 0d
Ditto to clerk and four turnkeys	£353. 6s. 0d
Ditto to matron of gaol	£30. 0s. 0d
Ditto to female turnkey	£31. 4s. 0d
Ditto to woman waiting upon prisoners	£13. 0s. 0d

Other expenditures included the baker's bill for the year (£33), the surgeon's (£80), clothing for the prisoners (£344 7s 8d) and repairs (£295 5s 1d).

In another account a claim had been made at the petty sessions in Kidderminster regarding a tailor called William Osborne:

> touching and concerning certain damage sustained by him and committed by persons having on the twenty fourth day of August last riotously and simultaneously assembled together and who did then feloniously demolish and destroy part of the dwelling house of the said William Osborne.

The justices of the peace had determined that damage caused amounted to 16s 6d. They asked that the treasurer pay the sum to William Osborne, together with £1 16s costs, and also 8s 6d to the high constable for his expenses.

There was a notification of a change to a footpath in Great Malvern. The footpath would be going through various properties so the chief constable had signed an affidavit to say he had contacted the people concerned, and that notices had been placed on the church door. Those with the lands affected had signed to say they had seen these notices. There was a plan to show where the footpath had changed.

Joseph Atkins had gone to the justices of the peace in Upton on Severn and reported that John Holmes of Birmingham had, on the 15 February 1831, been witnessed as being 'a hawker and trading person going from town to town and travelling in England' selling 'hardware and Japan goods' in Little Malvern. John Holmes pleaded not guilty but he was found guilty and fined £10. Punishments were written out, signed and sealed, such as this following example:

> Be it known that on the fourth day of February in the year of our Lord one thousand eight hundred and thirty one at the township of Stourbridge in the county of Worcester Sarah Keenan late of the township of Stourbridge in the said county was convicted before me the Reverend Joseph Taylor clerk one of his Majesties Justices of the Peace in and for the said county of being a Rogue and Vagabond within the intent and meaning of the statute made in the fifth year of the Reign of his Majesty King George the fourth entitled 'An Act for the punishment

of idle and disorderly persons and rogues and vagabonds in that part of Great Britain called England' (that is to say) for that she the said Sarah Keenan did upon the twenty seventh day of January last have in her custody and possession a certain crow, jack or implement at the township of Stourbridge aforesaid with intent feloniously to break into a dwelling house warehouse coachhouse stable or outbuildings against the statute in that case made and provided for which said offence the said Sarah Keenan is ordered to be committed to the house of correction at Worcester in and for the said county there to be kept to hard labour for the space of six weeks. Given under my hand and seal the day year and at the place first above written.

The justices of the peace also liased with the overseers of the poor regarding certain cases:

John Graves overseer of the poor of Mathon in the said county of Worcester maketh oath that he is acquainted with Ann Badham of the parish of Mathon, single woman who hath lately sworn before one of his Majesties Justices of the Peace for the said county that she was then with child and that the said child was likely to be born a bastard and to be chargeable to the said parish of Mathon and that Francis Jones the younger of the parish of Colwall in the county of Hereford wheeler had gotten her with child. And this deponent further maketh oath that he saw the said Ann Badham on Sunday the second day of January instant and she was not then delivered of the said child.

Sworn before me one of his Majesties Justices of the Peace for the said county of Worcester this 4th day of January 1831. James Graves, witness – E Sandern.

To his Majesties Justices of the Peace for the County of Worcester assembled at the General Quarter Sessions of the Peace holden for the said county on the 3rd day of January 1831 – Pursuant to the statute in that case made and provided, and in consequence of the above information this day made on oath before me one of his Majesties Justices of the Peace for the said County I do hereby certify the same to you to the end that the recognizant entered into with sureties by the above mentioned putative father may be reputed to the next general Quarter Sessions of the Peace to beholden for the said county given under my hand at Worcester this 4th day of January 1831 – E Sandern.

Petty Sessions

There were additional sessions held between the quarter sessions which dealt with minor matters, these were known as petty sessions.

A rule book for 1859 in Worcester Family History Centre lists the petty sessions held where and when:

Bromsgrove – every Tuesday
Droitwich – every alternate Friday
Dudley – every Monday
Evesham – every alternate Monday
Great Witley – last Monday in the month
Halesowen – every alternate Tuesday
Kidderminster – every Thursday
Northfield – the first Friday in the month
Pershore – every alternate Thursday
Redditch – when necessary
Stourbridge – every Wednesday and Friday
Worcester – every alternate Tuesday
Upton on Severn – every alternate Thursday

There were also petty sessions at Stourport, Tenbury and Great Malvern but no definite day was put aside for sessions there.

A look at the local paper following the particular day a session took place will give a small report of who appeared there and what cases were heard. For instance the *Bromsgrove, Droitwich and Redditch Weekly Messenger* for Saturday, 16 January 1864 gave the following report:

Petty Sessions, Tuesday – Before Capt. Bourne and John Webster esq.
Henry Webley charged Thomas Taylor with threatening to do him some
grievous bodily harm on the 4th inst.

However on examination Henry had said that he was not afraid of Thomas
any more so the case was dismissed. In another case:

James Saunders, nailer, of the New Buildings was in custody charged with
stealing one Guernsey cotton shirt the property of his father; William
Saunders.

Here, William did not press charges so the case was dismissed.

The other case ended with the accused being committed to Worcester to
await trial at the next quarter sessions. Heber Keep had been charged with
stealing gold worth £20 from his brother Kenaz Keep. His sister-in-law had
found Heber in the house rather the worse for drink, and later her husband
mentioned that the £20 was missing; when asked if he had the money
Heber ran away. A policeman was called and Herber was found in a public
house 4 miles away. There was no record of him at the next quarter sessions
so perhaps his brother relented after he felt his brother had been punished
with a short stay in the county gaol.

In the *Evesham Journal* of Saturday 18 August 1860, a report appears of
the petty sessions at Pershore on Tuesday 14 August. A Mr E Smith had been
summoned before the overseer for non-payment of Poor Rate. The amount
owing was 16s 10½d and it had been due since the previous October. The
defendant had argued that he had left Pershore two weeks after the charge
had been due and therefore felt he should not have to pay the full amount.
The bench demanded that, although he should pay the full amount that day,
they asked that five-sixths would be refunded to him. The overseer agreed
to this.

Meanwhile, at the Evesham petty sessions on 16 August 1860, Charles
Baker had been charged with 'running away from the parish of Bengeworth,
leaving his wife and family chargeable thereto'. Charles admitted the crime
and said 'it was a drunken freak'. He was given a sentence of one month

in the house of correction. William Williams, a hawker, admitted to being 'drunk and incapable in Cowl Street this morning'. He was fined 5s. A Bengeworth nailer was before the court for having assaulted his wife in a drunken quarrel. However Mrs Freeman asked that her husband 'might be forgiven'. Nathan Freeman was discharged with a caution and told to 'take the pledge'.

Bishops' Transcripts

There may be times when you cannot find documentary record of the event you are looking for. Perhaps there is a gap in the register for some reason. It is now that you will find the bishops' transcripts helpful.

The bishops' transcripts (BTs) were an annual list made by the vicar or his churchwardens and sent to the bishop or diocese, usually at Easter. These do not always contain all the information a parish register does, but they are particularly useful if the actual parish register is difficult to read. In Worcester Family History Centre there are quite a few for the counties of Warwickshire which fall into the diocese of Worcester. The Bishops' Transcripts were abolished in 1837 when civil registration began.

In the 1800s William Avery's book *Old Redditch* referred to 'one of our Townsmen' being required to 'produce the register of his birth'. He sought in vain for it and had to get certificates from the doctor and the nurse who were present at his birth. After some time discovered that he was the last person to have been christened in the Old Abbey Chapel, and the then clerk – who was a fish-hook maker – had, owing to the scarcity of paper, used leaves from the register to wrap up 'dabs' of hooks for the factory.

Looking at the registers from Redditch the baptisms do indeed end in 1805, although there is a separate book for 1807–1812. But it is quite evident from the microfilm that there are some pages ripped out: the tears are visible.

There is a comprehensive index to the BTs in Worcester Family History Centre. However, unlike the parish registers, all the parishes are grouped together for one year. This means searching through numerous microfilms unless you are sure about the year.

Maps and Enclosures

The Enclosure Act

Before the eighteenth century the English countryside largely consisted of open fields, common land and heaths. Although the common land was owned by the lord of the manor, the inhabitants were allowed to graze their animals on it. Farmers cultivated narrow strips of land separated by lines of grass on open fields. The old feudal system of working two-thirds of the land and leaving one strip fallow, then rotating the system over a three-year period, had been introduced by the Normans following the invasion of 1066 and was still in use.

But by the mid-1700s this method was considered out-dated and uneconomical. As new machinery was being invented, it was felt that farming methods should fall in line with the use of these new machines. Farmers wanted to be able to farm their own land in their own way, using different types of machinery as they wished; and so the idea of enclosure (also known as inclosure) became popular. Beginning in the 1760s, farmland began to be enclosed and prosperous tenants employed hired labour: it was soon realised that these methods resulting in better crops. Enclosing the fields in which the animals roamed was also showing a reduction in the spread of disease.

There now followed over 5,000 acts of Parliament, affecting over 7 million acres of land. Narrow strips of land were consolidated into separate farms owned by one farmer, who could then divide his land into fields enclosed with fences, hedges and ditches as he pleased. The first enclosures were made as joint decisions by the whole of a given village, but gradually landowners took control and enclosure was enforced by the submission of a bill to Parliament. By 1801 this process was becoming so complicated that the General Act of 1801 was passed. Commissioners were then employed to make the decisions of what land was to be enclosed and how. These decisions were recorded in an enclosure award, and an enclosure plan was then drawn up by a surveyor.

Unfortunately, not everyone benefited from enclosure. Those who farmed a small strip of land often lost that strip and became labourers working for a meagre wage. A small farmer found it expensive to erect the required fences; at the same time, with the invention of machinery for such things as spinning and weaving – which had been their winter 'home' industry – they began to loose work. The result was that they were bought out by richer farmers and so larger estates began to appear across the country. For the farmer, the choice was either to work as a labourer on land he had once owned or move to the towns to work in industry. Not only did the shape of the countryside begin to change, but the towns and cities grew.

To benefit best from the available information on an enclosure you need to view both the plan and the award. These often come together in the same book but can occasionally be held separately. The plan is very similar to a tithe map with all the fields being numbered. However, the owner's name is written across the particular group of fields he was responsible for. A second page will list the owners and the names and numbers of the fields. For instance the enclosure plan for Salwarpe in 1813 lists a Thomas Callow as an owner. His fields are:

173 – Builder's Brickyard
174 – New Mill, house
175 – Garden
176 – Mill Meadow
177 – Paddock
178 – Part of orchard

The award includes details of all relevant landmarks within the parish (i.e. 'Description of the public carriage, roads and highways') and their numbers in the plan and the direction they take, where the roads join each other and the properties where the junction or crossroad is. It also lists the 'appointment of private roads, bridge ways and footpaths'. Roads and bridle paths were to be a 'breadth of twenty feet'. Public and private footways 'of the breadth of four feet'. Private roads were usually those driveways which led to a farm and private footways were paths leading to cottages.

There was also a list of parcels of land which had been sold for building on. And there was a written statement as to where the fences were to be erected. The awards are very descriptive as to the parcel of land involved, the cottages or dwelling houses which were situated on them, and to whom they belonged. For example:

> Unto and for the said Matthew Wilson his heirs and assigns all that piece or parcel of land situate on Newland Common containing twenty eight perches (including the private road over the same) bounded on the south by the said Huddington Road and on all parts and sides thereof Brick House Gate and by the homesteads belonging to the said Matthew Wilson and Joseph Wythes respectively.

On the plan a small corner of land is marked as being awarded to Joseph Quarrell. One of the fields in this piece is numbered as 350. Looking on a sheet attached to the plan you will find this field listed which, among others, has been awarded to Joseph Quarrell:

Joseph Quarrell – Allotments in exchange
357 – In Parting Meadow
358 – In Parting Meadow
359 – In Parting Meadow
344 – Ridge Pit
345 – Long Ground
347 – Above Ridge Pit
348 – Old Leys
349 – Barn Piece
350 – The Sling
353 – Part of Homestead

Joseph Quarrell and Sarah his Wife
352a – Part of the Long Sling – One Newland Common

355 – The Four Acres

356 – The Two Acres

357 – New Orchard

358 – Cow Pasture

380 – Wild Duck Piece

381 – The Seven Acres

382 – Newland Field

383 – Newland Field

Reading through the award book you will find the statement made by the commissioner regarding these various pieces, for example:

Unto and for the said Joseph Quarell his heirs and assigns. All that piece or parcel of land situate on Newland Common containing ten perches

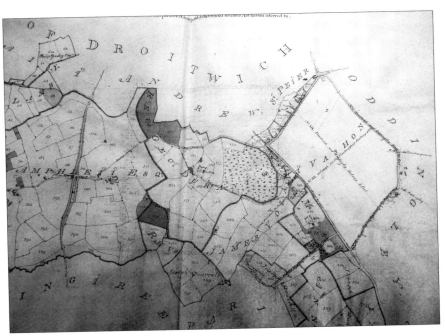

Enclosure Plans for Salwarpe show how the land is divided. Note in particular the fields belonging to Joseph Quarrell. The old thoroughfares can also be picked out and compared with today's roads.

bounded on the north by the Martin Husingtree and Oddingley Roads and on all other parts and sides thereof by lands in the parish of Oddingley.

All that piece or parcel of land containing two acres and seven perches part thereof belonging to Mrs Betty Chance and the other part thereof to the Rector as his sixty sixth and sixty seventh allotments therein before mentioned and described in exchange for the pieces or parcels of land and herediments belonging to the said Joseph Quarrell hereinafter described and which are allotted and awarded in exchange to and for the said Betty Chance and the rector respectively in manner hereinafter mentioned.
All that piece or parcel of land being the sixty fourth allotment hereinbefore made to the Rector called the Sling containing thirty six perches bounded on the North west by the remaining part of the said piece. And all that piece or parcel of land situate on that part of Newland Common containing three acres in exchange for the piece or parcel of land and hereditaments therefore belonging to the said Joseph Quarrell and Sarah his wife and hereinafter described allotted and awarded in exchange to and for the Rector in manner hereinafter mentioned. And I the said commissioner do hereby order direct and award that the part of the piece of land called the Sling herein before awarded in exchange the said Joseph Quarrell and Sarah his wife from the residue of the said piece shall be made and for ever thereafter kept in repair by and at the expense of the said Joseph Quarrell and Sarah his wife and the owners for the time being of the said piece of land so hereby awarded in exchange to the said Joseph Quarrell and Sarah his wife.

It all seems a rather elaborate piece of writing just to say you can have this piece of ground, or you can have this one. But that is the fun of family history – trying to read through all the old jargon.

Tithe Maps and Apportionments

Other maps of interest to family historians are the tithe maps and apportionments. Originally tithes were a 'payment in kind' to support the church and its incumbent. They amounted to one-tenth of the profits of a person's land or property. Everything was included – crops, milk, eggs, wool, animal stock. In fact some vicars carried their rights too far.

A well-documented murder which took place in Oddingley in 1806 concerned the local vicar, the Reverend George Parker, who was murdered by a carpenter from Droitwich who had been 'hired' by a group of farmers. George Parker had been a little too eager to receive his one-tenth – even down to demanding one-tenth of any hedge cuttings.

As the feudal system declined with the introduction of enclosure, it also became necessary to improve the system of paying tithes. Farmers began to feel that payment in money was a better option, but not all churches agreed with that idea, so the Tithe Commutation Act of 1836 was passed. This brought in an annual rent on land which was reviewed regularly to fall in line with inflation. Tithe commissioners were appointed to oversee the change from tithes to the rental agreement and three copies of the apportionments and maps were made. One copy went to the Crown and can now be viewed at the National Archives. Another copy went to the diocese and the third copy went to the churchwardens. It is the churchwarden's copies that are now found in Worcester Family History Centre.

The tithe apportionments and maps available at Worcester Family History Centre were made according to the situation on 16 February 1843. They have been filmed alphabetically and, depending on the size of the parish, the number of pages the map is spread over differs. However, they must not be taken as 100 per cent accurate. Normally they are approximately 25in to 1 mile, but this ratio can differ.

The following example is from Alvechurch:

Know all men by these Presents whereas I, Charles Pym, have been duly appointed and sworn as assistant tythe commissioner according to the provisions of the Act for the Commutations of Tithes in England and Wales and have also been appointed to ascertain and award total sums to be paid by Rent charges instead of tithes in the parish of Alvechurch in the County of Worcester.

The map of Alvechurch covers six pages. It shows where the boundaries are with its neighbouring parishes – Cofton Hackett, Kings Norton, Bromsgrove and Tardebigge. The roads and canal are clearly marked, together with the direction they are taking when they leave the parish; the road through Hopwood states 'to Kings Norton'. Two branches left will take you to either Longbridge or Northfield. The canal disappears into the tunnel before leaving the parish; this too is clearly marked, and is shown as going to Birmingham. The maps can easily be compared with a modern map of today as to existence of roads, where development has taken place and what is still there.

Buildings are marked as to shape and size but are not named (apart from the church). The sizes and shapes of the fields and buildings are clearly defined, each with its own number. You will need to know these numbers when looking at the apportionments to find out who owned the property. Deciding whether to look at the tithe map first, or the apportionment, is purely a personal decision. If you are interested in the layout of the parish – who owned what building or parcel of land, or who lived where – then look at the plan first and note the numbers within the area you are particularly interested.

If you are looking for where an ancestor lived, use the tithe apportionments first. However the apportionments are listed alphabetically by ownership, so if your ancestor rented a building or land you will need to go right through the apportionment looking for his name under the occupiers' column. And remember it was not uncommon for someone to rent a house from one person and parcels of land from another; do not stop when you find the name you are looking for, as there may be more to discover.

The plot number is given in the next column, and another column will give a description of the land or premises such as house and garden, shop, orchard, plantation, pleck, allotment or hop garden. Then the 'state of cultivation' is shown; arable, mead, pasture or wood. The quantities in statute measure, and the amount of rent and to whom payable, complete the apportionment.

As an example: buildings are shown in the centre of Alvechurch as being numbered 55, 54 and 56. Looking through the apportionment number,

56 is identified as being a house and garden owned by Richard Boulton and rented by Charles Fisher. John Newbold owned both 55 and 54. He occupied number 55 which was the Old Swan Beer House and Garden. Thomas Warner occupied number 54 which was a house, stable and garden.

Even the canal and its banks were included, the owner and occupier being the Birmingham and Worcester Canal Company. The descriptions for the parcels of land were given as 'canal and towing path', 'part of reservoir' and 'canal towing path and bank'; no rent or tithe was paid.

Ordnance Survey Maps

The Board of Ordnance was established in the 1500s to supply weapons and ammunition to the army and navy. Its headquarters were in the Tower of London. In the late 1700s there was a worry that, as the French Revolution developed, there may be a threat to England and a possible invasion. So the Board of Ordnance was given a new task: to make a survey of the south coast, which began in June 1791. However the Map of Kent was not published until January 1801. This was followed by the Map of Essex.

During the next twenty years a third of England and Wales had been surveyed at a scale of 1in. The Ordnance Survey Act of 1841 gave the surveyors the legal right to enter private land for the purpose of making inspections. That same year, a fire broke out in the Tower of London; although all the records and instruments were rescued, there was a need to move into larger premises. The Ordnance Survey now moved to Southampton.

In 1863 the mapping of rural land on a scale of 6in and 25in to 1 mile, and built-up areas on a scale of 10ft to 1 mile was approved, but it was not completed until 1895. In 1935 the National Grid Reference was introduced.

It is the 1882–1890 edition that is held on microfilm at Worcester Family History Centre. There is a hardcopy map of Worcestershire to tell you which number map you need for the area you are looking for. The maps themselves are not a lot different from today's. They are also very useful to plot the direction an enumerator travelled while taking the 1881 or 1891 census, or just to compare a place as it was then.

Manorial Records

Manors vary in size and often there may be more than one manor to a parish. A small manor will be made up of just one farm and a few cottages; a larger one may include more than one settlement, farms, common land and woods. A typical medieval manor consisted of the church, a vicarage, a manor house, a mill (to grind corn), tenants' cottages, and the three open field systems; divided into strips and separated by lines of grass.

The lord of the manor employed various people to undertake the running of the manor. The steward managed the estate as a whole and presided over the manorial court. The bailiff assisted the steward and also received the rent from the tenants. The tenancies were arranged through the reeve. A hayward made sure all the fences were in good repair and looked after the common stock of animals, and the constable maintained law and order.

The manorial court was the lowest court in the country and dealt with very minor offences committed within the manor itself. Worcester Record Office holds a large number of the rolls (minutes) for the manorial courts of Worcestershire.

If you are looking for records pertaining to a particular parish, you will find that many are filed with the family papers of a particular lord of the manor. *The Victoria County History of Worcestershire* lists many manors and their owners, but the record office has a good card index specifically for manorial records listed by parish in alphabetical order. Manorial records can give an abundance of information for both family and local history.

The availability of records can span 400 years from the 1400s up to the 1800s, but be prepared to read through documents with no punctuation. The Court Leet Rolls are an example of such records. In many cases these are scrolls of continuous paper that have to be rolled and unrolled carefully, but Worcester Record Office does supply leather paperweights and beads to keep the documents held down in the right place. One roll for Tardebigge covers the period 24 October 1777 to 27 October 1787. Fourteen jury members had been sworn in: 'The names of the jury who are sworn to enquire as well for the King as the Lord of the said Manor.' The lord of this manor was Lord Windsor, earl of Plymouth.

The proceedings began with the presentation of a new reeve: Joseph Compson of the parish of Tardebigge was to stand for a year together with a 'reeve in elect' who was George Webb of Feckenham. Walter Byron was elected as the constable for 'Redditch Liberty', Henry Harbage as 'headborough' for Webheath and Richard Chambers as constable for Tutnell. They elected William Lucas and Henry Millward who were both 'of Redditch' as bread weighers and ale tasters for the parish of Tardebigge.

It was agreed that a fine of 10s 6s would be imposed on anyone who 'let a pig or pigs go unrung after a weeks notice of being asked to do so'. They then got down to the business of tenancies.

Rowland Berkeley of Cotheridge had sent a letter with his solicitor, Charles Welch, requesting that he be allowed to become the tenant of Dyal House. The tenancy included its barns, stables and outbuildings and parcels of land. In response to this request 'the said Lord by his steward aforesaid granted the premises'.

The next case was as follows:

To this court came Edward Williams a copyhold or customary tenant of this manor in his proper person and in open court surrended by the Rod into the hands of the said Lord by his steward aforesaid according to the custom of the said Manor all that customary or copyhold messuage or tenement leantoes stable and building court and close containing about an acre (beit more or less) together with ways waters water courses timber trees fruit trees hedges ditches mounds fences common profits and apportionments whatsoever to the said messuage or tenement and premises belonging or in anywise appertaining situate and being at the lower end of Redditch at or near a place called or known by the name of Pidgons Bridge within this manor and now in the several tenures of possession of James Millward Jnr William Bolton and John Oakes And all his estate right title interest property claim and demands whatsoever of in and to the same premises or any part or parcel thereof to the use and behoof of the said Other Earl of Plymouth his heirs and assigns forever.

Another case involved the tenancy of someone who had died:

> To this court came Kitty the wife of George Silvester of Bromsgrove in
> the county of Worcester gentleman the only daughter of and heir at law
> of William Lucas late of Redditch within this manor snuff merchant
> deceased one of the copyhold or customary tenants thereof and desired
> to be admitted tenant of all that copyhold messuage or tenement and
> farm commonly called or known by the name of Boxknott together
> with an allotment of new inclosed common land all situate and being
> in that part of the parish of Tardebigge which lies in the county of
> Worcester with four several closes and pieces of arable land meadow and
> pasture ground containing in the whole by estimation eighty eight acres
> of land or thereabouts be the same more or less with all houses outhouses
> buildings barns stables gardens orchards holdyards ways waters water
> courses profits priviledges heredits and apportionments whatsoever there
> unto belonging or in anywise appertaining and now in the possession
> of Jeffs to whom the said Lord by his steward aforesaid granted the
> said premises and she hath seizin thereof by the Rod according to the
> customs of the said Manor to have and to hold the same premises unto
> the said Kitty Silvester her heirs and assigns for ever. At the will of the
> Lord nevertheless according to the customs of the said Manor by the
> rents heriots suits of court and all other services thereof due and of right
> accustomed And the said Kitty Silvester is admitted tenant to the said
> premises and gave to the Lord for a fine one silver penny But her fealty
> was respited by reasons of her coverture.

So here you have some assistance with your family tree if you are having
trouble proving certain individuals. You now have proof that Kitty Lucas,
who was the daughter of William Lucas, married a George Silvester and
went to live in Bromsgrove.

Searching the wills in the Worcestershire index a will was found for
William Lucas. It was dated 16 August 1782. In it, after various small bequests,
he left 'all the rest and residue of my real and personal estate monies chattels
and effects unto my daughter Catherine Lucas.' The will was proved on

17 February 1786. By now, Catherine Lucas had married George Silvester: 'Catherine the wife of George Silvester (formerly Catherine Lucas) the daughter and sole executrix within named appeared and was sworn in common form.'

Again, going back to 1766, the rolls include a list of tenants who had died and their lands had been passed on to their beneficiaries.

> We present that since the last court died Mr John Sanders copyhold of this manor seized of three copyhold estates within this manor and we find his daughter Elizabeth Sanders the wife of James Sanders his heir ought to be admitted and find three heriotts due to the Lord.

Incidentally, the person writing the rolls all those years ago did not make a mistake with the names. There is a marriage in Tardebigge in 1755 for a John Sanders and an Elizabeth Sanders. Further investigation may show that they are cousins – something quite common in those times.

If a court book is available this can also be quite helpful in tracing lineage, as it will list the occupants of various tenancies in the parish over a period of years. It was quite usual for children to take over their parents' property, so again may help prove parentage where no baptism has been found, or if there is more than one to choose from. If you are lucky enough for your ancestor to have held some land, a tenancy agreement passed from father to son will prove parentage.

For example, the following concerns property in the manor of Cropthorne described as 'one messauge and two acres of domestic land and one acre of land at Black Pit with the appertenancies'. On 17 October 1795 the 'lives in possession' were William Loxley and Mary Walker. Through the first half of the nineteenth century ownership passed through the family:

On 8 October 1817	William Loxley and Thomas Walker
On 24 October 1820	Thomas Walker and William Walker
On 22 October 1833	William Walker and Richard Loxley jnr
On 21 October 1851	Richard Loxley and Henry Roberts

The parish registers for Copthorne show that William Walker was the son of Thomas and Mary Walker.

In some cases the court book can just give you an idea of who lived at a certain property before and after your ancestor. Finding a record such as the following could also help to prove or disprove if a burial you have found is that of your relative:

One messuage and one yard land called Chapman late of William Bayley one messuage and half yard land and a quarter of an acre of land formerly Folliott and late of William Davis one toft and one yard land formerly Rea with the appertenancies with the Manor aforesaid. Lives in possession:

June 4, 1787.	Esther Haywood, John Timms
October 17, 1813.	John Tymbs, George Bushell
February 13, 1835.	John Tymbs, Corbett Holland

Notice the different spelling of Timms, both written in different handwriting!

If a property takes you into the years of the census, then a census record could be used in conjunction with the court book. The court book may also describe how land was split and enclosed after the enclosure acts, or may give the ages of those living in a property:

a messuage with several parcels of land in Crowle.

October 11, 1774.	Philip Brooke aged 35, edward Walton aged 39, Robert smith aged 37.

All of which may be helpful information to the family historian. The steward's accounts can further show the work undertaken by this position. In most cases they made arrangements for the transfers of tenancies from a deceased tenant to others – sometimes other members of the family – which again can be useful to your research.

Other manorial papers are bundled together and boxed under certain BA numbers. These boxes can contain a variety of documents, for example one such box (ref: 009:1 BA2636. Bundle 153) for parishes which belonged to the manor of the bishop of Worcester, contained complaints regarding the building of the canal. One petition dated 1 May 1786 was from the 'owners and occupiers of mills, forges and lands on Belbroughton, Barnett and Broadwater brooks against the bill for making a canal from Stourbridge Navigation to the Severn, near Worcester'.

The properties included thirty-six forges, ironworks and paper and corn mills which lay on these brooks and which were below the line of where the canal was going to be built. Extensive trades were carried on here which was supported by the brooks and large sums of money had been spent in establishing the works. They were concerned that the canal would take away a lot of the rainwater and the brooks would eventually run dry. There was a similar petition from the 'owners and occupiers of several corn, cotton, needle, paper, cloth, leather and other mills upon several brooks and streams in and near the towns of Bromsgrove and Droitwich in the county of Worcester.'

There were papers concerning the building of a bridge over Hawford Brook on the road from Kidderminster to Worcester. A builder called George Perry had given his estimate of £250. The bridge would span 37ft and would be 21ft in length. The road was to be a length of 18ft 6in and the arch would extend 91ft. The walls would be of a good hard stone.

Another bridge was also causing a manorial debate. It was undecided whether a bridge at Wyre Piddle in the Manor of Fladbury should be repaired or rebuilt. It was noted that:

this bridge was never any other than a horse bridge for the convenience of carrying bags to market in a flood time and is as good a bridge for that purpose and in as good repair as any bridge in the county. But Mr Anthony Craven a waspish Justice of the Peace who perhaps passes that way one in a year happened to come there in his coach at a flood time and because he could not get over with his coach is resolved to have it made a bridge for coaches and carts and was the ground of this indictment which is prosecuted by him for no one else complains the bridge being in very good repair and never otherwise than a horse bridge. But if he can prevail with the Bishop Dean and Chapter to make him a coach way we shall not be displeased thereof.

Sometimes documents can give quite an insight into the history of a property and its occupants. In the manor of Hartlebury in the seventeenth century was a property which had various papers attached to it. It was initially described as 'a messuage or cottage situate and lying in Hartlebury near the Lord Bishops park with a garden adjoining containing two perches'. Occupancy progressed thus:

October 4 1632. Elizabeth Tomlins. Edmund Waters
April 21 1668.   Jane Edwards, widow. Admitted to popism.
                 Emanuel Smythe jun
                 Margaret Laycon, wid
                 Elizabeth Smythe

July 20 1688   John Inett, yeoman in popism
                 John Webb, Rowland Webb, Jane Webb sons and
                 daughter of Rowland Webb of Great Witley. In trust
                 for said John Inett

This copy was first granted by Bishop Thornborough to his keeper Edwards and renewed after the King's Restoration when the castle was in ruins. I account this cottage to be fit for one else but the keeper of the park and therefore I will never renew the copy to the tenant. But I will give the full worth of it for the Bishop's use if the tenant will part with his copy.

Bishop Lloyd did not renew the copy to the tenant. On 20 October 1701 a court record showed that the widow of John Inett, Elizabeth, who was referred to as 'tenant in possession' together with John and Rowland Webb and Jane Phillips, surrendered all their interest in the property. In 1709 paperwork showed that:

The Bishop ought to have passage out of his parish towards Kidderminster through the grounds let to Hill into the lane that leads up to the Highway. The Bishop has always had a gate out of the park into those grounds but Hill has made a ditch before it. This should be remembered at the next renewing. 1709, October 26. He was here to renew but I refused it unless he would submit to a clause for reserving of a passage for me and my successors through that ground as oft as there should be occasion.

Oddments Among the BAs

There is extensive information to be found among the original records, papers and documents which are held in Worcester Record Office at County Hall. With the help of these papers you will find that family history and local history can easily be entwined.

On the shelves in both Worcester Family History Centre and Worcester Record Office are box files containing numerous card indexes. These are known as the bulk accessions. You can go to the Bs and find parishes such as Beoley, Berrow, Birtsmorton etc., clearly indicated with markers. Under these parishes all the cards are again alphabetical – deeds, guardians of the poor, poor law records, as well as individual family and property names. However, these individual names and properties are also indexed under their own letter; for instance, the references for the Vernon family of Hanbury will be found indexed with the Vs, or in the Hanbury section, under V.

A 'BA' number is given on the card and in most cases a small description of what the record contains. However if you then look in the BA volumes for that number, a more detailed description will be given. You will often find one BA number will contain numerous separate parcels, so you will need to decide which parcel contains the document you would like to look at. Others may contain just one item, or one separate parcel.

An example of one such BA is that for the Davies family. The parcels contain photographs, letters, diaries, newspaper cuttings and other papers belonging to this local family from Elmley Castle – it was donated by one of their descendants. The newspaper cuttings are from both foreign and English newspapers and cover the years 1901–1965. There are travel photographs covering 1928–1934 and diaries from the 1920s. Other photographs go back to the late 1800s and early 1900s.

Other BAs contain deeds, leases and indentures for properties in Clent and Belbroughton dating from the fourteenth century to 1557. Old reports dating from 1881–1931 have been deposited by the original Worcester Gas Board in another parcel. The Women's Institute has donated scrap books collected in the 1960s. There are plans for the building and repairing of a bridge in Doddenham covering the years 1858–1956. Whilst the field message book of a First World War officer, used for manoeuvres in France in 1915, has been donated by his family. Nearly 300 years of history for a boot and shoe manufacturers from Worcester can be followed in one BA. The parcel includes their deeds, abstracts of titles, assurance policies and receipts for the years 1616–1899.

A large BA which is divided into numerous parcels contains about 1,400 items. These include plans of local farms, letters, accounts, valuations and sale catalogues for the Bentley Estate near Redditch from 1827–1966. Other personal papers are those of a William Hunt and include his diaries, deeds, licences, assignments, articles of partnership and other papers dating from 1860–1888.

Not all the documents are original manuscripts. One BA contains copies of letters and other papers which belonged to John Feckenham (1518–1585), the abbot of Evesham. The photographs of the originals were taken by record office staff in 1968 at the National Archives and the British Museum.

A large majority of references for Worcester Record Office, and other record offices, can be found on the website www.a2a.org.uk. There is a comprehensive search facility and it will give you the BA number, parcel number and reference number and save you from thumbing through the record cards when you visit the record office.

Even if you don't find a diary written by your ancestor, a diary written by someone else living in their town at the same time, will give you an idea of what may have been going on; small snippets that may not have reached the newspapers. The Reverend William Lea, who was the vicar of St Peter's, Droitwich, wrote his diary from 1849 to 1887. In it he talks of many local people and local events, as well as national and international events, wars and politics. And if you want to know what the weather was like or how the crops did, then you will find out here. Here is a selection of various examples:

September 25, 1849. Thursday was observed as a day of fasting and humiliation to avert the visitation of cholera which has appeared among us. Some few cases have appeared in 'The Vines' but they came I am informed from Stoke, where several cases have appeared.

July 1850. The Stoke Company have left the salt works at Droitwich and Clay & Newman have taken them in hand and as their first act have dismissed all the saltwomen. A petition had been sent to them requesting them to dismiss all under 30 and never admit anymore but they have preferred to do away with The Evil at once. Preached a sermon in St Peter's on the subject in showing our gratitude was due to them for the courage they have taken. The late company had for some time past refused to admit any new female hands in consequence of the representations made to them.

November 1, 1854. Reports of a battle at Balaklava in which our light cavalry were almost destroyed.
November 18, 1854. A terrible fight at Inkerman. The Russians assaulted our line on the 5th, surprised us and were only driven back after six hours. Severe fighting – losses were said to be severe. A collection was made from house to house. £17 raised in the parish.

[1878] We had a singularly mild winter. No frost to speak of – in the Spring we had cold winds and excessive rain which lasted throughout May till the second week in June. The weather then suddenly changed to great heat which lasted through July. The crops of hay are very large and were got in in excellent condition, and in a good soil the prospects of harvest are not bad. Fruit crops have been generally good – but gooseberries, apples and pears are below average – currants and strawberries above – plums are good though many have fallen off.

[1885] Gladstone's ministry which came in five years ago with a majority of 120 were out-voted on a major point and immediately resigned. The general impression was, and I believe it to be true, that they were purposely beaten in order to prevent disruption of the cabinet from internal dissensions. It was believed that Chamberlain and Dilke differed from the rest of the cabinet on the Irish question.

The indexes for the school records are kept in indexes, alphabetically, for the town the school is in. It is doubtful you will find any registers but you will probably find log books which will tell you about the day-to-day running of the school. Other items you may find are the governors' meetings minutes or the school account books.

School logbooks can be interesting to read as they show the lessons our ancestors were taught and the tests they took. However, you will only see your ancestor's name amongst the pages if they were exceptional or, unfortunately, if they were exceptionally bad. You may discover who their teacher was, when their holidays were, if the school was closed at any time, and the prevailing weather conditions.

Summer holiday was then often referred to as harvest holiday. Children earned money helping with the harvest and comments written by the headmaster show that if the harvest was early they missed school, and if it was late they did not go back at start of term. Illness and epidemics often closed the school; children were sent home if there was an outbreak of smallpox in their house to prevent it spreading. The weather affected schools in much the same as it does today. In many cases children had to travel quite a distance to attend school and heavy snow would certainly hamper their attendance.

These examples from a school log book for Powick shows you the sort of things you may expect to see when reading through one of these books:

[1863]

January 20. Examined 1st class, 15 children. Arithmetic as far as compound multiplication. Dictation, reading, on slates – 10 commendments.

January 21. Examined 2nd class, 17 children. Arithmetic – addition, subtraction, multiplication tables, dictation, reading. Scripture – write an account of the Prodigal son and life of John the Baptist.

January 22. Bad weather meant small school.

January 23. Continued bad weather and small school.

[1873]

August 22. Kept children in at their lessons for 4¼ hours this morning and then told them that there would be 5 weeks holiday

September 29. Monday – commenced school this morning with 93, which is unusually good.

December 10. Louisa Knott having 14 mistakes in a moderately easy piece of dictation of course was punished like several of the others, when she started for home as her mother told her to go home if the master punished her. I cannot punish one and let another off with more mistakes when I know that it could have been done very much better.

[1882]

17 May. Albert Marshall and Arthur Kilvert climbed over the girl's gate and left the premises to go bathing and to play truent.

July 30. Tuesday. A half-holiday. The children went to the exhibition at Worcester through the kindness of the vicar who with myself and teachers accompanied them.

August 10. Complaint by Mr Turner of the children entering his fields and treading down his corn on coming to and from school causing great damage. 25 children had been guilty of it names follow – Louise Bird, J Knott, L Knott, E Watkins, M Baylis, L Gorle, M Pollard, J Shepherd, M Smith, E Jones, A Pollard, A Pullen, J Jones, F Beard, L Jones, H Price, A Ward, S Leek, C Matthew, C Poultry, W Lawrence, R Smith, G Pollard, H Knott, F Jacobs.

[1883]

February 27. I tore out of Mary Harris exercise book a leaf on which her home lessons for the evening were written, because there was written upon it some very obsene expressions which were brought to me by a boy and which she had allowed her brother to write at home.

Military Records

If you ask around your relatives you may find photos in the family of your soldier ancestors going back over 100 years ago. Many soldiers had their photos taken before going to war as gifts for other members of the family. Any visible badges and insignia will point you to their regiment and rank, which will help when searching for their records or the history of the regiment. If a soldier was killed his wife, or parents, would often have memorial cards printed to be sent out to family and friends. Some of these may also still be in the family somewhere too.

The majority of army and other forces' records from the First World War are held at The National Archives at Kew. These are classified under their own codes: WO for the war office; ADM for the admiralty; AIR for the Royal Air Force (from 1918); and ZJ/1 for *London Gazette* announcements, such as citations and awards. However, the service and pension records are not complete as many of them were destroyed by bombing during the Second World War. All the medal rolls index cards are available, but these give little information apart from regiment and service number. All soldiers who participated in a given expedition were given a campaign medal.

Records for the First World War can also be found at www.ancestry.co.uk. Due to the quality of the papers there are a few differences with the amount of detail and information they give. If you do find your ancestor's service record it can be quite informative. If he married during his years of service a copy of the marriage certificate is often lodged with his papers, or at least the date and place. Children he had will be listed, together with their dates of birth. You will see the dates he was abroad and where he was sent. If he was injured, you will find out when and where.

For example, Alfred Duffin of Hunt End, Redditch, was 37 years 5 months old when he enlisted on 5 February 1916. He was a needle-maker and was unmarried. His next of kin was his father, John Duffin, who must have died during the war as his name was crossed out and changed to Alfred's mother's name of Temmia. Alfred was 5ft 9¼in tall, weighed 194lb and had a chest measurement of 40in, expanding to 44in. He had no distinctive marks. He was first placed with the reserves until June 1917 and then posted to the Royal Garrison Artillery as a gunner on 26 June 1917. As part of the page has been damaged and the writing is very faint it is difficult to read where he was posted, but on 30 November 1917 he was declared 'missing'. Just over a week later, on 8 December, he was reported as being a prisoner of war in Germany. His mother was informed on 21 January 1918. He survived to be repatriated and returned home to Enfield Road, Hunt End on 24 April 1919. His medical history shows that he was in the Connaught Hospital from 6–13 August 1917 with diarrhoea.

Sometimes a record will belong to a soldier who was in the army long before this war broke out. Arthur Harris was a labourer living in Kidderminster when he enlisted on 5 March 1901 aged 18 years 2 months. He joined the 6th Battalion Worcester Regiment after being a member of the Worcester Militia from 25 May–19 October 1900. His father was Lewen Harris of 22 Waterloo Street, Kidderminster. He had three brothers: Harry, Walter and Lewen. On 4 October 1912 he married Mary Fletcher at Kidderminster Parish Church and they had two daughters – Charlotte May born 9 September 1914 and Lily Maud born 11 February 1917.

At 5ft 4in tall, Arthur weighed 115lb and had a chest measurement of between 33–34½in. His hair was brown, and he had brown eyes and a fair complexion. He served in South Africa from 5 March 1902 to 19 December 1902, and India from 20 December 1902 to 8 January 1909. The rest of his twelve years of service was spent in England. However, during that time he had not been a model soldier. He was arrested twice as his records show:

4 April 1910. In civil custody. Convicted and sentenced by civil powers to seven days hard labour for being drunk and disorderly.
2 December 1912. Convicted and sentenced by civil powers to fourteen days hard labour for a misdemeanour.

Arthur re-enlisted on 14 June 1913 and was posted to the reserves. He was discharged on 2 January 1919 having spent only a short time in Salonika.

Sometimes a soldier was discharged as being 'no longer physically fit for war service'. The medical reports show different conditions such as cardiac irregularities and complaints of giddiness, shortness of breath and someone who had been off-duty on numerous occasions although he had not been admitted to hospital. Perhaps he was also a 'physically weak looking man.' Very often the causes were due to contracting typhoid fever while in the army.

If a soldier's injury was enough to warrant him a pension you will find his papers among the pension records. Here you will find the details of his injuries, the results of the medical examinations he had had, and if his request for a pension was successful. It is hard to believe but when men complained of having recurring chest and breathing problems, which were no doubt due to the conditions in the trenches or from being gassed, their teeth were examined. If it was found that these were bad, the problem was put down to poor dental health and the soldier was refused a pension.

The papers for the pensions are the same as the normal soldiers' papers except they have the additional details with regards to the type of disability, the medical reports and the award, if any was given.

Even soldiers who had been wounded would not necessarily get a pension after the war. A soldier injured in Ypres on 9 January 1915 with shrapnel wounds to the hand, arm and shoulder was, although immediately discharged from the army, considered 'quite recovered from the effects of the wounds and that his earning capacity is not lessened.'

Of course soldiers did receive pensions. Bertram Durose was gassed on 28 September 1917 and spent almost four months in various army hospitals. He complained of coughing and sweating at night and headaches. He was awarded 5/6 per week. Another soldier received a gunshot wound to the right leg and right buttock on 1 June 1916. A medical report in

June 1919 stated that his leg was weak after a long walk. He was awarded £52. Presumably this was a one-off payment rather than a pension. In 1916 Percy Durose suffered a malaria attack in Salonika. After the war he was still suffering from short bouts of malaria but in 1920 the medical board thought these attacks would only last twelve months and awarded him 8s to expire on 1 February 1921. However, a second award of 7/6 was given at that time to expire on 31 January 1922.

Some soldiers who had served as regulars before the war could be registered as Chelsea Pensioners and receive a 'daily' income – '29½d a day from 1 April 1919 to 3 January 1930. Attaining age of 55 on 4 January 1930 subject to an extra 5d a day then when 65 another 4d a day.' Soldiers with children were often given a pension for them until they reached the age of 21. James Durose had three children and had been posted in France for three months in 1916. Despite having suffered from asthma since the age of 12 he had still been considered fit for the army. However in December 1917 he was declared physically unfit – 'not the result of, but aggravated by active service conditions.' He was awarded 6/3 for his three children.

To search for the death and final resting place of a soldier ancestor there are two options. The Commonwealth War Graves Commission's (CWGC) website asks for a surname and initial. The results page then brings up all those with that initial. The record for each name gives the rank, service number, date of death, age, regiment, nationality, grave or memorial reference and the cemetery. If you click on the individual's name a further link takes you to details of the cemetery, its location and its history and number of graves. You can also access photographs and maps of the cemeteries and read the lists of others who are buried there.

There is also a list of the 'Soldiers and Officers Who Died in Great War'. This is available on CD and at www.findmypast.co.uk; it is based on an official casualty list published in 1921. Searching its index will give similar results to the CWGC, and both directories complement one other.

The National Roll of Honour, also at Findmypast, will tell you about your ancestor's background in the armed forces. The idea behind these volumes, which were published by The Publishing Company when the war ended, was to include a biography of all men and woman who were involved.

However, the roll is not complete and Worcestershire is not covered. But if your ancestors originated from Worcestershire and strayed over the border into Birmingham you may find them or one of their descendants in the Birmingham volume.

If you are not sure if your ancestor took part in the First World War check the electoral registers for 1918. The absent voters section will list the serviceman aged twenty-one or over for each town.

After the Great War, as it was known then, many war memorials began to spring up across the country. Some were just a symbol of respect for those who had died; whereas some listed the names of those who had died from that town or village. A national list of war memorials and their inscriptions is being undertaken at present. The website for this is www.ukniwm.org.uk. You can search for a surname and the results will give you the inscription and where the memorial which bears the inscription is. You can also search for a particular place or building where a memorial may stand. It is very much an ongoing project at time of writing.

At www.warmemorials.org you will find details of those memorials which are currently receiving renovation. A charitable organisation, the War Memorials Trust, is working to protect and conserve our war memorials as part of our culture. They monitor the condition of a memorial and assist local groups in repair and conservation.

Other soldiers' records are kept at The National Archives. However, the website Findmypast is adding military records at regular intervals, in particular Chelsea Pensioners' records. Other sites which give a history into the Worcestershire regiments are www.worcestercitymuseums.org.uk (who also have permanent displays in respect to the Worcestershire soldier), and www.worcestershireregiment.com, which has facilities for an archivist to undertake searches in their archives for a fee.

The Worcestershire Militia was formed on a regular basis in 1770. Before then it had been a body of part-time soldiers selected randomly from various parishes and trained in their spare time, to be called out when needed during wars and invasion crises. They were called out during the Armada, after the exposure of the Gunpowder Plot and during the Civil War. Their roots go as far back as Saxon times. The original barracks were in

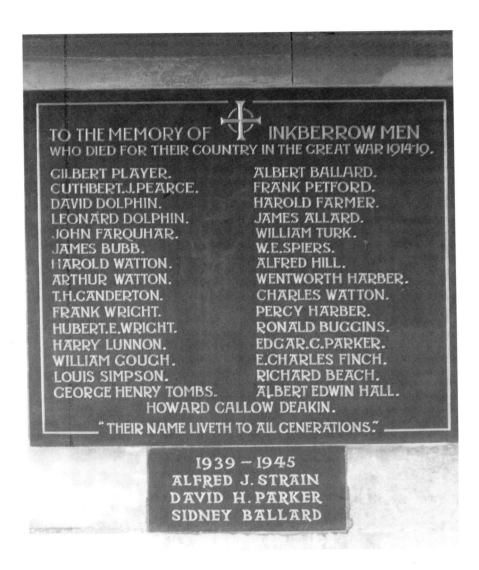

TO THE MEMORY OF ✝ INKBERROW MEN
WHO DIED FOR THEIR COUNTRY IN THE GREAT WAR 1914-19.

GILBERT PLAYER.	ALBERT BALLARD.
CUTHBERT. J. PEARCE.	FRANK PETFORD.
DAVID DOLPHIN.	HAROLD FARMER.
LEONARD DOLPHIN.	JAMES ALLARD.
JOHN FARQUHAR.	WILLIAM TURK.
JAMES BUBB.	W. E. SPIERS.
HAROLD WATTON.	ALFRED HILL.
ARTHUR WATTON.	WENTWORTH HARBER.
T. H. CANDERTON.	CHARLES WATTON.
FRANK WRIGHT.	PERCY HARBER.
HUBERT. E. WRIGHT.	RONALD BUGGINS.
HARRY LUNNON.	EDGAR. C. PARKER.
WILLIAM GOUGH.	E. CHARLES FINCH.
LOUIS SIMPSON.	RICHARD BEACH.
GEORGE HENRY TOMBS.	ALBERT EDWIN HALL.

HOWARD CALLOW DEAKIN.
" THEIR NAME LIVETH TO ALL GENERATIONS."

1939 – 1945
ALFRED J. STRAIN
DAVID H. PARKER
SIDNEY BALLARD

Inkberrow. This plaque is inserted in the lynch gate of the church and bears the names of those in the village who were killed.

There are two surnames which appear twice on the First World War plaque – Dolphin and Wright – and one which appears three times – Watton. In a small place like Inkberrow it is reasonable to infer that those sharing a surname were related.

Also note the names Ballard and Parker, which appear on both the First World War and the Second World War plaques.

St George's Square, although the soldiers could be billeted anywhere around the city. Norton Barracks, about 2 miles south-east of Worcester, was built in 1878, and in 1881 the militia became the 3rd and 4th Battalions of the Worcester Regiment. In 1900 they expanded to the 5th and 6th Battalions.

Farrington's Regiment of Foot was formed in 1694 by Major General Thomas Farrington. In the late 1740s it became known as the 29th Foot Battalion. It spent most of its time abroad so had no base in Worcestershire until 1877, when it was also billetted at Norton Barracks. In 1881 it was formed into the 1st and 2nd Battalions of the Worcestershire Regiment.

The Worcestershire Volunteer Force was formed in 1798 along with many others across the country, but was disbanded and reformed on several occasions until 1859, when it became a permanently established unit. In 1908 the Territorial Army was formed and the Worcester Volunteers became the 7th and 8th Territorial Battalions.

The Worcester Yeomanry Cavalry was formed in 1794 and, apart from a short break from 1827–1831 due to lack of funds, existed until 1899. Its duties were usually civil ones, when it would be called out to help with riots and strikes.

There is a variety of personal papers in the bulk accessions in Worcester Record Office and a small amount of books on the shelves in Worcester Family History Centre. Using the a2a website and searching both the words 'militia' and 'military' and choosing Worcester Record Office as the repository, there are over 200 results for Militia and thirty-one for military. The records held at Worcester Record Office include diaries, letters and scrapbooks, as well as occasional lists of personal for certain years.

The Worcester Exhibition of 1882

No visitor to Worcester of late years can have failed to notice the spectacle of a colossal building turned to little or no account. Walking from the railway station into the city down Shrub Hill, or Shrubs Hill as it used to be called, it was melancholy to gaze on the multitudinous broken panes and torn gratings of a pile which should have resounded with the clatter of hammers and the noise of machinery. Time has brought its compensation. A change has come over the spirit of the dream: and now that immense structure is the scene of a minature representation of all the characteristic industries of a busy English county and the home of rich treasures of art gathered from the country grange, the nobleman's gallery, the national collection and wherever beautiful objects were to be found.

This was the opening statement made in the *Berrow's Worcester Journal* of 22 July 1882 regarding the opening of the Worcester Exhibition. This exhibition was not considered comparable with the Great Exhibition of 1851, but it gave a good platform for the manufacturers of Worcestershire to show off their merits.

It had been suggested for a long time that Worcester should hold its own exhibition; many places around the country had done so since 1851. But it had only been decided a few months previously, and credit was given to Mr H. Day, Mr S. Smith and Mr C.M. Downes for having set the stone turning.

The Earl Beauchamp had been made president of the committee and £1,600 was promised as a fund by various backers. In the end £6,200 was raised.

Five sub-committees had been set up: Fine Arts Section; Industry; Historical; Building and Finance; and Catalogue, Advertising and Entertainments. Then it was decided that the old Engine Works would be a suitable place to house the exhibition. With its vast size and height, its layers of blue, red and white bricks, circular headed windows, noble entrance and its flanking tower, it was an ideal location. The building had been built in 1864 to house the Worcester Engine Works Company. In 1872 it had been acquired by the West Central Waggon Company Ltd. for three years. After that it had remained empty, with parts of it being occasionally used by various companies. But on the whole, as the opening paragraph from the *Berrow's Journal* states, it had been left to fall into decline.

In February 1882 the architects Messrs H. Rowe & Sons prepared a report showing what repairs needed to be undertaken. Several tenders were submitted, but the job was awarded to Messrs Binnian & Son of Kidderminster, who gave an estimate of £995. The roofs were repaired, the walls painted, the windows glazed and parts of the floors were replaced or repaired. An orchestra to seat 230 was erected and a new organ, which was being built for the church of St Mary Magdalene, was loaned. Messrs Hardy and Padmore supplied an iron veranda for the entrance. The eventual end cost of restoring and adapting the building was £2,000.

The exhibition opened on Tuesday 18 July 1882. Mr Norman May of Malvern was employed as the official photographer and exhibitors were instructed only to show their goods and the prices and not to 'solicit' the public. To cover the bare walls of the main hall, carpets from Kidderminster were hung. These were supplied by Tomkinson & Adams, J. Brinton & Co., Wodward Grosvenor & Co., H.R. Willis & Co., H.J. Dixon & Sons and R. Smith & Sons. A bronze group entitled 'A Moment of Peril' took centre stage. It had been sculptured by artist Mr Brook and depicted an Indian being attacked by a huge serpent. Also around the room were hung portraits of famous Worcestershire people from throughout history.

Showcases contained examples of china from the Worcester Royal Porcelain Company, glass from Thomas Webb & Son and gloves from

Dent, Allcroft & Co.; other exhibitors included Hardy & Padmore, Edward Webb & Son and W B Williamson & Son. A large block of salt, carved with elephants and crests, stood in the room. Messrs Hingley of Netherton exhibited an enormous anchor and chain weighing 6 tons and there were iron workings from Lord Dudley's works.

In the Fine Arts and History room there were paintings from Holman Hunt (his famous 'Shadow of Death'), T.F. Dicksee, B.W. Leader, Haynes Williams, Sidney Cooper, J.C. Hook, G.F. Watts, T. Woodward, David Bates, W.A. Firkins and a view of Powick Bridge by H.H. Lines. Local artists included Mr Brandish-Holte, Mr Gyngell, Mr Hooper, Mr Noke, James Callowhill, Scott Callowhill, Mr Rushton and Mr Bibbs. Many works of the old masters were loaned from the galleries of the Marquis of Hertford, Earl of Coventry, Earl of Dudley, Lord Northwick, Lord Lyttleton, Lord Windsor, Sir E.A.H. Lechmore, Mr G.E. Martin and Mr C.W. Lea. There was also a display of the sculptures by local artistes Forsyth and Hadley.

The History Department contained old books and charts donated by Earl Beauchamp, Dr Hopkinson and Mr R.W. Binns. There were displayed several works of Oswen, the first Worcester printer who had settled in the city in around 1548. Another case contained items that had once belonged to Charles I including his christening robe. Outside the room was a collection of Jacobean furniture including a spinet made around 1656 and a spinning wheel. Carpet looms belonging to Messrs Tomkinson and Adams and Messrs Brinton & Co. of Kidderminster demonstrated the process of how carpets were made, from a bobbin of wool right through to the finished article.

There were also small workshops showing the works of the Royal Porcelain company and Messrs Dent, Allcroft & Co. Messrs Mckensie & Holland had erected a railway signal cabin to demonstrate the workings of the system. Whilst the businesses displayed in the industrial section included: Scott & Oram, silk merchants and drapers of Victoria House, Worcester; Josiah Stallard & Sons, brewers; and Whitgrove & Sons carriage makers. The exhibition remained open for three months, closing on 18 October 1882. In those three months 222,807 people had visited the exhibition and a profit of £1867 9s 6d had been made. This profit went towards building the Victoria Institute in Foregate Street. Today, this building houses the library and museum.

The Towns: their Industries and their People

If you want more out of your family tree than just names and dates, then family history research must go hand-in-hand with local history research. There is nothing wrong in including a history of the places where your ancestors lived, the people they may have known, their neighbours, historic events which may have occurred in their lifetime, the church they married in and had their children christened and where they are buried. Knowing the details of a certain town may explain why an ancestor left there or why he moved there.

Alvechurch

The Saxon church made of wood is no longer standing today, but it was a Saxon lady, Aelgiva, that gave Alvechurch its name. There is mention of a priest here in Domesday Book but it was the thirteenth-century bishop of Worcester who helped with the establishment of the town. He had a palace built here of which only the moat and fish ponds remain. Because of the arrival of this eminent person the town was now granted a weekly market and an annual fair, and was given the status of borough.

In the fourteenth century half the population died of the Black Death and rumour has it that their bodies were buried outside the village in Pestilence

Lane. However when building the M42, surveys of the area were undertaken and nothing was found. Hopwood Services now stands on this spot.

For the next 400 years, up to the eighteenth century, the village was a predominantly agricultural community. Hiring fairs were held every October where workers would parade themselves in front of the local landowners who were looking for workers. The lucky ones would be assured of a full year's work.

After the Worcester to Birmingham Canal was built, a new generation of boat builders began to establish themselves and several wharves appeared. With the building of the railways the people were now within easy reach of other industries and most were either employed in the needle industry of Redditch or the nail industry of Bromsgrove.

Directories of the 1800s described Alvechurch as an extensive parish which included the hamlets of Rowney Green, Barnt Green, Hopwood, Forehill, Lea End and Withybed Green.

The present church, St Lawrence, was consecrated in 1239 but a large part of it was renovated n the late 1850s.

Belbroughton

Belbroughton is mentioned in Domesday Book but there is also a mention of it in Saxon rolls of the ninth century. It was the centre for scythe making; the majority worked in the blade mills, grinding and sharpening the edges of the tools after they had been forged by the smith. The main manufacturers were Waldrons of Clent, who were based in Belbroughton for about 100 years from the late 1700s to the 1870s. They were then bought out by Isaac Nash of Galton's Mill, who undertook the welding and the plating. He was now able to undertake all the processes in making complete scythes and Nash Works established themselves in the centre of the village. In 1881 he was stated as employing 105 men and 6 boys. The mill closed in 1970.

The church, Holy Trinity, was described in directories of the 1870s as being an old stone building with a tower, a spire and six bells. The chancel was paved with encaustic tiles. *The Victoria County History of Worcestershire* suggests that it dates back to the twelfth century.

Beoley

A small parish of only a few hundred it was a very rural community, containing just arable land and woodland. The church of St Leonard, according to *The Victoria County History of Worcestershire*, was built during the twelfth and thirteenth centuries and a chapel was added by Ralph Sheldon, lord of the manor, in the late 1500s. This contains the tombs and memorials to members of the Sheldon family.

An 1876 directory describes Beoley as 'a picturesque village' and the trades people listed are mainly farmers – although there is a needle and fish hook manufacturers called 'Beoley Mills'. In March 1885, however, the village was to hit the headlines. The *Worcester Daily Times* for Monday 2 March 1885 reads:

> One of the most shocking murders that has of late years been committed in this county took place in the dark hours of Saturday morning, near Weatheroak Hill, about three miles from Kings Norton.

James Davies had been in the police force for five years and was stationed at Beoley. He was a tall and powerful man but his body was found 'much mangled' lying in a 'great pool of blood' which had flowed from a wound in the head. It was a quiet, lonely spot and he had probably lain there for some hours. He was last been seen by a fellow policeman at 1.00am, and it was now 8.30 in the morning. It appeared there had been a desperate struggle; his truncheon, helmet and whistle were found strewn across the lane. To punctuate the gruesome scene, footprints of the assailant were found astride the body; he had made a final cut across the policeman's throat as he lay dying. A nearby farm had been broken into and six hens had been taken. As feathers were found nearby it was assumed James Davies had apprehended the poacher.

The grave of the murdered police constable James Davies stands close to Beoley church, whose parishioners tend it. The murder was a notable crime at the time and Davies' story is still told to new recruits today.

Suspicion immediately fell on a well-known poacher called Moses Shrimpton who had only recently been released from prison and was known to be living in Birmingham. He had many offences to his name including an attack on a policeman in 1868. Originally from the area, he was known to frequent Beoley on occasion.

On the Monday morning officers made their way to Birmingham and an address at 9 Bartholomew Street. Shrimpton was found here with marks of blood on his clothing and a small cut to his head which could easily have been made by a truncheon. His knife had recently been cleaned. He insisted he was not guilty, saying 'I know nothing about it. I can prove where I was Friday night'.

At the Worcester spring assizes the defence for Moses Shrimpton suggested that as it was one of their own who had been murdered the police were determined to bring someone to justice. But the prosecution had their evidence. Footprints led from Wheatheroak Hill Farm, where the chickens had been taken, to Icknield Street. Matching footprints were seen together with Davies footprints, suggesting that he had apprehended Shrimpton and had begun to march him down the lane. Feathers had been found in Shrimpton's pockets which matched the breed of chickens stolen from the farm, and a watch like the one James Davies owned, which was missing, had been offered for sale by Shrimpton. Unfortunately the man who had bought the watch, fearing the consequences, had destroyed it. Shrimpton's lady friend was seen waiting in Birmingham station for the arrival of the Redditch train at 8.45 that morning which suggested that Shrimpton had been in the district the night before.

The jury only needed five minutes to bring their verdict of guilty and Shrimpton was executed at Worcester on Monday 26 May 1885. The grave of James Davies lies in Beoley churchyard and is still cared for and kept in good repair by the parishioners. A memorial also sits at the place James Davies died and new recruits are still taken to see it as a reminder of the risks taken by the police.

Berrow and Birtsmorton

In 1876 Berrow had a population of 426 and Birtsmorton 292; but did you have ancestors there in 1780? Did they know the Gummery family or were they related to their neighbours, the Player family who found the bodies of the Gummery family?

Mr Player had been awoken at four in the morning by strange noises in the house next door and on going round had found the bodies of Edward Gummery, his wife Elizabeth and their 8-year-old daughter Ann in one bedroom, and Elizabeth's brother-in-law, Thomas Sheen, in the other bedroom. All had been brutally murdered.

Edward was lying on the floor, his back ripped open, bowels hanging out and one arm almost severed from his body. His wife lay beside him, her head hacked to pieces. Their daughter's throat had been cut. Thomas Sheen was still lying in his bed, his head sliced open.

No-one was ever charged with the murder although two men were arrested having been found a short way from the scene with blood on their clothes. But they were part of a group of travelers, and the others in that group gave them an alibi. There was no apparent motive for the crime. There was money still in the house; none had been stolen. Edward was described as a poor but honest and industrious worker and both he and his wife as being inoffensive and harmless; it was unlikely that they had quarreled with anyone. There was talk that Elizabeth had witnessed the destruction of enclosure fences and reported it to the authorities; perhaps it was an act of revenge.

Was it something to do with Thomas Sheen, and had the Gummerys been murdered because they had woken and witnessed his murder? After all, Thomas was still in his bed and Edward & Elizabeth were out of theirs, which could point to him having been murdered first – unless, of course, he was a heavy sleeper.

The case was never solved. Nearly thirty years later, an old man was admitted to hospital with a fractured leg. Throughout the night he babbled in a delirious state about a murder he had taken part in. Someone who remembered the Gummery murder recognised some of the details and pressed him to say more. But he died the next morning, taking the secret to the grave with him.

Bewdley

Bewdley was an important inland port and the evidence of its wealth is in the prominent bridge which was built by Thomas Telford. The town is mainly Georgian but a few Tudor and Jacobean properties still exist.

The town of Bewdley didn't become a parish until 1853. Previously it belonged to the parish of Ribbesford and the old Norman church stands a mile away. On the outskirts is Tickenhill Palace where Prince Arthur (Henry VIII's brother) was married to Catherine of Aragon. However, she was absent as the marriage was by proxy.

The earliest record for the district is in Domesday Book for a settlement at Wribbenhall situated on the eastern side of Severn. In the fourteenth century it became known as Beau Lieu (beautiful place). The tanneries in Bewdley date back to the Middle Ages. The bark for the fires was supplied from the nearby Wyre Forest.

The Wyre Forest was abundant with oak, birch and ash and supported many industries. The heavy timber was sent for shipbuilding; small branches were used for besom making, basket making, bean sticks and hurdles; and the bark was used in tanneries in Bewdley. The bark was stripped in the forest by groups of women who would walk miles each day to the felled trees. They would sit around the tree stripping the bark in semi-cylindrical pieces. Even into the 1920s, bark-peeling was an important occupation in Bewdley employing over forty people. However, by the start of the Second World War it was dying out and only eight people were involved. A use was even found for the ferns in the forest: they were used in packaging fruit.

Charcoal burning was also an occupation to be found in the forest. It provided the fuel for iron furnaces. The charcoal burners worked in rough tent-like structures made of tarpaulin sacks with pits inside. Covered with turf, the wood smouldered for four or five days. It was then dampened down and the charcoal removed.

Known as the Far Foresters, the people of the Wyre Forest lived like gypsies. They were lawless and survived by poaching and sheep stealing. There is a well known story from 1833 of three overseers from Bewdley who went from hut to hut checking who was living there. They were met with verbal abuse and told if they came back again to bring their coffins with them.

Blockley

During the eighteenth century, when wool was in decline, the silk industry became fashionable. In 1884 there were six silk mills in Worcestershire which employed around 600 people in total. They mainly worked as throwsters;

Blockley, a town nestled in the Cotswolds – boundary changes mean it now belongs to Gloucestershire. It once contained thriving silk mills which provided an abundance of work for its population.

people who twisted the silk fabrics into thread for the silk ribbon makers in Coventry.

The industry began to decline in the late nineteenth century after a levy on imported silk was imposed. The largest of the silk mills was Westmacott Mill which has now been developed into flats and called Blockley Court. Two other mills became piano-making factories.

The Church of St Peter and St Paul is an old stone building dating from the Middle Ages, with parts showing Norman construction.

Bredon

In the summertime on Bredon
The bells they sound so clear
Round both the shires they ring them
In steeples far and near
A happy noise to hear.

The first verse of *A Shropshire Lad* by A.E. Housman gives a view of a summer's day on Bredon Hill. Roman earthworks have been found here and it is said that eight counties can be viewed from the top of the hill. The hill forms a natural divide for the Cotswolds and the Vale of Evesham.

In the town itself there is a medieval tithe barn made from fourteenth-century Cotswold stone. It is cared for by the National Trust.

Broadway

A place for tourists; they throng here in their hundreds during the holiday season. Above Broadway, high on the hill, is the Broadway Tower, a folly built by Lady Coventry in 1790 which was the holiday home of William Morris. Morris was born in Walthamstow, London in 1834 and was educated in Oxford where he met Burne-Jones and Rossetti and formed the pre-Raphaelite movement known as The Brotherhood. In the 1850s he became interested in wall papers, carpets and tapestries; his designs can now be found in many stately homes.

Bromsgrove

In AD 909 the town was called Bremesburh; in Domesday Book it is referred to as Bremesgrave, Breme meaning 'famous person' and 'grave' a fortified clearing in a forest. Who the famous person is remains unclear.

Medieval times saw Bromsgrove a prosperous centre for the woollen trade, but nailmaking became its leading trade in the seventeenth century.

Bromsgrove is described in a directory of 1876 as a large market town containing many excellent houses and shops. The streets were well-paved with a supply of water from pumps and lighting by gas. The cemetery covered several acres. There was a grammar school which had been founded by Edward VI in 1553. And a monthly cattle fair and a weekly market on Tuesdays for corn and vegetables.

The parish includes the hamlets of Burcot, Dodford and Sidemoor. Catshill became a parish of its own in 1843 and the hamlet of Bourneheath joined this parish.

Nail making was introduced to the area by the Huguenots and quickly centralised in Bromsgrove. Although the nearby towns of Dudley, Stourbridge and Cradley were also involved in nail making. In 1750 1,000 nailers were employed in Bromsgrove, by 1861 this figure had risen to 2,500. At first the principal nail makers of Bromsgrove were grouped around the High Street but during the 1800s the trade expanded out to the neighbouring hamlets of Catshill, Bourneheath and Sidemoor. In fact, when the trade in the centre of Bromsgrove began to decline in the 1880s, Catshill began to prosper and continued until 1914.

The nailers worked in their own cottages, which were usually rented from a nail master. They supplied their own benches and tools, but the nail master provided the forge and bellows. Whole families: husbands, wives and children (as young as 7) worked in the cottage and life was hard. Often they did not earn what they should have; the 'middlemen' who collected the nails from the worker were known to be crooked and many tampered with their scales to reduce the amount of money they paid out.

In the hamlet of Catshill the nailmakers' cottages were built around 1830. They were square and built of red brick with one room up and one room down. The cottages often had only one window, at the front only. One small square outbuilding in the yard was used as the forge. Every Saturday nailers collected their orders and iron rods from one of the warehouses – either Banners in Meadow Road (Dog Lane), Waldrons in Golden Cross Lane or Parry's in Church Road. The nail manufacturers listed in the 1876 directory are:

James Green & Co.
E. Hadley & Son, Catshill
Holmes & Hickton, Sidemoor
T. Parry & Son, Catshill
Perkins & Laughton
S. & J. Price
Scroxton & Brooke
Joseph Witheford & Son

The church of St John the Baptist was built over a period of three centuries – the twelfth, the thirteenth and the fourteenth – but is believed there was a church here before then in the eleventh century.

Droitwich

Patients suffering from rheumatism, gout, sciatica, dyspepsia, and other disorders which spring from a deranged system, may here find relief and generally perfect cure.

This is how a trade directory from the 1870s advertises the benefits of the Brine Baths in Droitwich.

The main parish for Droitwich is St Andrew's, which originally dates from the thirteenth century. However, a fire at the end of that century meant that it was mostly rebuilt in the fourteenth century. St Nicholas church was built in 1876 on the Ombersley Road. About a mile south-east of the town is St Peter's, another medieval church.

There is evidence of a settlement here in the Iron Age and the relics found suggest the salt springs had probably already been discovered. A Roman fort stood here on the top of Dodderhill in AD 47–70. St Augustine's parish church now stands here, which in parts is Norman. The parish church of St Andrew's is Anglo-Saxon.

Sainae was founded by the Romans but Droitwich derived its name from the old English words 'wiches', meaning salt pits, and 'dryht', meaning lordly. This described the quality of the brine which was very pure and high in sodium. It is thought that the Romans were the first to discover salt in Droitwich. The word 'salary' comes from the Latin 'salarium', the allowance of salt given to the Roman legionaires. When the Roman Empire ended the salt trade continued to be a slow-growing industry and certainly was not at its height until the early 1800s. Although in 1086 Doomsday Book showed that there were ten brine pits and 230 salt pans in Droitwich, and that it was the main salt producing town in England.

Droitwich was given a charter by King John in 1215 but little is mentioned regarding the salt industry between 1215 and 1539. In 1539 papers state that there were three springs (or wells) in the town, with a search for a brine-pit taking place. It is recorded that in 1727 deep borings were being made to produce a stronger burst of brine. Salt now began to be produced at a higher rate.

In 1762 the Salt Company met with James Brindley to discuss plans for the building of a canal from Droitwich to the River Severn. The River Salwarpe had been used for carrying the salt, but in the summer it could be too shallow and in the winter it often flooded. Work began on the canal in 1768 and it was finished in 1771.

In the early 1800s a Cheshire brine smelter discovered numerous brine springs in nearby Stoke Prior and by 1828 the industry had spread out to

Once the home of the Nash family, St Peter's Manor stands next to the church. In the early 1780s Dr Nash wrote two volumes of *The History of Worcestershire*, still valuable volumes for family and local historians today.

the outskirts of the town. At its height there were thirty-two recorded wells situated in Dodderhill Street, Friar Street and High Street.

In 1850–51 the brine pipe riots took place. There were too many salt makers and the larger ones were trying to oust the smaller ones. Unfortunately, this was made easier by the fact that the smaller salt workers were not within easy reach to the brine. The 'Company' had their brine-pits at their works, but nearly all the other individual salt-makers obtained their brine from pits further away from their works. The 'Company' thought they could install their brine pipes anywhere, as long as they didn't interfere with the surface. However they did not worry if they interfered with someone else's pipes and fights often broke out between rivals.

On one particular occasion a number of men cut off the pipes of another salt worker, therefore stopping the brine reaching Mr Ellins' salt works. He tried to re-lay his pipes with the help of friends but men from the larger salt works continued obstruct him. As this happened many times between the salt workers, poor Mr Ellins' incident appears to be one of many.

Droitwich remained a close-knit community of salt-workers well into the early twentieth century. People from other parts, even those from as nearby as Worcester, were regarded as foreigners. It is evident from the gravestones and parish registers that there was much inter-marrying between local families. Droitwich's most notable employer was John Corbett – 'The Salt King'. He took over the salt works in Stoke in 1853 and soon expanded them. He was a respected member of the church and held high morals regarding female labour.

Previously, there had been no set hours for women working in the salt works, and they worked alongside men doing the same jobs. These jobs were undertaken in hot, steamy atmospheres and involved loading and moving the salt; they wore the minimum of clothing. The brine was pumped into reservoirs then carried to large pans heated by fires. The salt particles formed from the evaporation, and left in the bottom of the pan, were dried in wooden boxes and then shaped into blocks. Men worked stripped to the waist.

John Corbett made the decision not to employ women in the salt works and to compensate a family for the loss of the wife's earnings; he increased the wages of the men. He also improved their working conditions. Women were allowed to continue packing the salt, but they were segregated from the men. From newspaper reports it seems that it had taken some years for this regulation to be recognised. A notice dated 24 December 1858 shows there were a lot of people trying to back the new conditions:

TO THE SALT MAKERS AT STOKE WORKS
The indecency and wickedness arising from the employment
of Women and Girls in Salt Works have become so bad
that it is considered a duty to God and Man to put an end to it.

NOTICE IS HEREBY GIVEN,
that after Friday next, the 31st December, 1858, no Women or Girls
will be permitted on these works.

It is earnestly requested that Salt Makers will keep their Wives at Home
to attend to their Children and Household duties

STOKE WORKS
December 24th 1858

An 1860 local directory does list other salt workers for Droitwich:

Bourne & Greaves, Hill End
Clay & Newnman, Droitwich
Joseph Ashby Fardon, Vine works, Droitwich
W. Noak & J. Cover, Droitwich

In 1900 Droitwich and Stoke Prior produced 170,000 tons of salt per
annum, and their combined works now belonged to the Salt Union Ltd,
apart from John Bradley and Messrs Boucher & Giles. *The Victoria County
History of Worcestershire*, published in 1912, says that by then there was only
one salt factory in Droitwich: the Covercroft Works.

The brine in Droitwich is said to contain 39 per cent salt – nine times
more than sea water. In 1823 a cholera epidemic erupted in the town. The
water was contaminated; people began bathing in a hot brine bath and
found their ailments miraculously healed. A local resident, Mr Gabb, built
the first brine bath in 1836 for the treatment of rheumatic and arthritic
patients. In 1870 it was taken over by Dr Bainbrigge and Mr Rock and
eventually bought by John Corbett. John Corbett also built the second
brine baths in 1888. Droitwich was now becoming a holiday resort for
the rich and famous who came to relax in the waters. Salt production
in Droitwich ended in 1922 but the popularity of the brine baths
has continued.

St Peter's Manor House in Droitwich was the home of the Nash family.
The name Dr Treadwell Nash will be familiar with local and family
historians as he wrote two volumes of *The History of Worcestershire* in the
early 1780s. These are available at Worcester Family History Centre and can
be an interesting tool to use as a reference guide.

Dudley and its Environs

The Saxons established the town of Dudley. Duddeley was named after the Saxon Lord, Dudo or Duddah, who cleared the forest (Duddah's Leah) and built the original castle. The present castle, although ruined, is from Norman times. It was slighted by the Parliamentary armies in 1647 and then became a residence. In 1750 it was damaged by fire and remained in ruins.

The world's first steam engine was made in Dudley in 1712 to pump water from Lord Dudley's mines, and it was here that the Industrial Revolution began. Together with its surrounding hamlets of Oldbury, Old Hill, Lye, Stourbridge and Halesowen, Dudley merged with other industrial towns across the border of Staffordshire to become a conurbation known as the Black Country. This land was soon covered with the waste and dust from the mines, and the air polluted with the fumes and smoke from the furnaces and forges.

The parish church is St Thomas' which stands on the High Street, but as the town developed it split itself into other parishes. Although the church of St Edmund's on Castle Street was built in 1724 it did not become a parish until 1844. St James' parish at Kate's Hill was also formed in 1844 – the church having been built in 1840. St Luke's on Wellington Road was the newest, according to the directory of 1876, having only been consecrated on 28 July 1876.

As far as Worcestershire is concerned the coal industry centres around Dudley, but is actually an extension of the South Staffordshire fields. A small field ran from the Wyre Forest into Bewdley and Arley, and a small field was also found and mined for a short time in the Lickey Hills, near the village of Rubery. The Pensax district of north Worcestershire was owned by the dean and chapter of Worcester. Coal was brought down the Severn and was also supplied to Droitwich for salt-boiling.

The first collieries (or coalerys as they were then called) began to appear in the 1700s. They were not very deep; even in 1835 pits went down no further than 450–600ft. In 1851 Dudley mined 700,000 tons a year and most of the works and collieries were owned by either the earl of Dudley or Cochrane & Co. A 1876 directory lists other colliery owners:

Garratt Shelah & Son
John Jones & Sons
Daniel Lowe
Richard Mason
Richard Mills & Co.
Phillips & McEwen
William Waterfield & Son

In the early years coal was worked like agricultural land, pits were regarded as part of the manorial estate with leases being let to tenants. Records show that coal was being excavated in Worcestershire in the thirteenth century but at that time wood was normally used for burning. Coal began to be used more as chimneys became popular.

The district also has seams of iron; the mineral seams of Worcestershire extend from those of the South Staffordshire fields. The main seams were found in Oldbury, Cradley, Stourbridge, Halesowen and Old Swinford. Iron has been mined for longer than coal and for many years wood was used to smelt iron. It was finding the coalfields so close to the surface which enabled the Worcestershire fields of coal and iron to be worked in conjunction with each other. Messrs Cochrane & Co. of Woodside in Dudley were connected to the iron industry as well as the coal mines. Other iron manufacturers in Dudley included:

William Crimes & Sons
George Henry Deeley
Johnson Brothers of Phoenix Works
John Jones & Sons
Homer Mountford
Arthur Nichols
Philips & McEwen
William Smith & Son
Westwood & Wright

Another firm in the Dudley area was Hill & Smith. Arthur Meredith was a clerk here in 1878 and every Friday he would go to the bank in Dudley to draw the workmen's wages. Enoch Whiston watched these weekly journeys from the window in a public house but on 6 December of that year he left the inn as the clerk was making the return journey. He shot Arthur in the head and ran off with the black bag containing £280 6s 9d (about £13,000 in today's money). When he was arrested and was told that Meredith had died, Enoch confessed, saying that he had not intended to kill him.

Evesham

Evesham was also established by the Saxons. The abbey, which was one of the largest in Europe, was founded by Egwin, the third bishop of Worcester, in AD 702. A local shepherd alleged he had seen a vision of the Virgin Mary. When the bishop visited the same site he witnessed the same vision and had the abbey built on the site. The shepherd's name was Eof and the name Evesham derived from the phrase 'Eof's ham' – a ham being the name given to homestead.

The town grew in importance under the Normans and the abbey became a popular place for pilgrims. It is now in ruins, a victim of Henry VIII's Dissolution of the Monasteries. The church, All Saints, is part Saxon and part Norman.

The battle of Evesham took place on 4 August 1265 between an army raised by Simon de Montfort and Henry III. A small number of barons had opposed the king and what they thought was poor government. They felt too much money was being spent on wars overseas so went to war in an attempt to force the king to accept more baronial council. At the battle of Lewes in 1264 de Montford triumphed over Henry, whom he now held in his custody.

The royal army led by Prince Edward (later to become Edward I) was much stronger than the force raised by de Montford, which was making its way to Kenilworth to link up with reinforcements. They met outside Evesham and a massacre ensued, with de Montford killed and his body mutilated. His torso ended up in a tomb in Evesham Abbey but other parts were sent all over the country.

Evesham is split between three parishes: All Saint's, St Lawrence's and St Peter's of Bengeworth. The town is largely Georgian in appearance, although some medieval buildings do still exist. A directory from the 1870s describes Evesham as clean, dry and well-paved, with gas lighting. The suburb and parish of Bengeworth was connected to Evesham by a bridge over the Avon.

From the mid-1800s a lot of the land had been converted into gardens, and many farms became orchards. As much as 3–4,000 acres of land was changed this way. There was also a thriving business in seeds and hops. The majority of women in Evesham worked in the glove industry; materials were sent out to them on a weekly basis.

The Vale of Evesham, with its abundance of fruit growing and market gardening, is found to the south and east of the town and includes the villages Middle Littleton, Bretforton and Cleeve Prior. Also included are Offenham and Badsey, which specialised in asparagus. Pea picking was also a popular occupation of visiting town and city dwellers. It gave them the chance to enjoy the fresh air of the vale and earn money as well.

The district supplied many places with their fruit and vegetables: towns as far away as London, Liverpool and Manchester; as well as those nearer to Evesham such as Tewkesbury, Cheltenham, Birmingham and Dudley.

The Lenches are north of Evesham and contains two parishes. Church Lench belongs to four settlements – Church Lench, Abbots Lench, Atch Lench and Sheriffs Lench – and stands on the ridge overlooking the Vale of Evesham. In Domesday Book the district belonged to the Abbey of Evesham. Rous Lench includes two settlements – Rous Lench and the hamlet of Radford. Fragments of carved stone found in the area would suggest there was a Saxon settlement here, although the church, St Peter's, is Norman. Rous Lench Court was owned by the Rous family who were parliamentarians. It is said that Oliver Cromwell dined here the night before the Battle of Worcester in 1651.

Feckenham

In the middle of the twelfth century Feckenham Forest covered most of Worcestershire. It stretched from Bromsgrove in the north to Pershore in the south, and to the city gates of Worcester in the east. But between 1229 and 1608 it became gradually smaller, and in a survey of 1608 the Crown decided to 'disafforest the forest of Feckenham'. Within twenty-one years Feckenham Forest had become common land.

The village of Feckenham stood in the centre of the forest between Alcester and Droitwich. It was a small Saxon settlement created on the salt way, originally built by the Romans. Until the late eighteenth century it was mainly an agricultural village but, when the needle and fishing tackle industries developed in nearby Redditch in the 1790s, the trade rapidly

A sleepy village, its populous once worked in the needle and fishing hook industries, largely working from their own homes. It originally stood in the middle of Feckenham Forest and still has a very rural feel to it.

expanded out to Feckenham as well. In fact, many of the needle makers who moved from Long Credon, in Buckinghamshire, to the Redditch area in the mid-nineteenth century settled in the Feckenham parish. Factories included John English & Co. and W. W. Gould & Sons. In 1906 in *The Victoria County History of Worcestershire,* George Webb and Sons of Feckenham Mills was said to be the oldest surviving firm in Feckenham.

The church of St John the Baptist dates back to the middle of the thirteenth century but, according to an 1876 directory, has been much altered.

Feckenham, although in Worcestershire belongs to the union of Alcester in Warwickshire and the parish includes the hamlets of Astwood Bank, Hunt End, Callow Hill, Ham Green and parts of Crabbs Cross.

Halesowen

The Saxons thought this spot on the River Stour a good place to build a settlement. They named it Hales, which means a nook or corner piece of land.

Until the mid-twelfth century Hales belonged to the Crown, but in 1174 Henry II gave it to his sister, whose husband was the son of Owen, prince of Wales. Eventually, but not until 1270, Hales-Owen took its name. King John gave his permission for French monks to build an abbey here in 1215. After the Dissolution of the Monasteries the abbey of St Mary's was given to John Dudley, the Duke of Northumberland.

Coal was found in nearby Hill in the early 1300s and at one time there were over 100 mines in and around Halesowen. Nails were also made here and in 1868 a company called Congreaves was manufacturing steel.

The church of St John the Baptist stands in a large churchyard and is of Norman origin, although there is evidence of a Saxon church being here.

Within the parish of Halesowen was the town of Cradley. Here was the extensive iron works of Messrs Evers & Sons who made anvils, hammers, anchors and chain cables. Harper and Moore manufactured firebricks and clay retorts. King Brothers were the proprietors of Stourbridge Clay and manufactured bricks and other fire-clay goods. Whilst the Cradley Colliery Company was in the centre of the town and in the north was the salt water spring called Lady Well.

In 1876 Halesowen was described as a large and sprawling parish. There were 12,245 acres and a population in 1861 of 29,293. The directory of that year lists the following iron foundries:

Colbourne & Somers, carriage iron forgers
Cartwright & Parkes, nail & chains
Homes & Hickton, nails, chains & cables

Hanbury

Hanbury is a quiet village and an extensive and fertile parish. It is famous for its hall, built in 1701 and once the home of the Vernon family. Edward Vernon had bought the manor of Hanbury in 1630. He was the son of Richard Vernon, who had been the rector of the village, and his descendants went on to become eminent lawyers. There are numerous family papers belonging to the Vernon family in Worcester Record Office which include many deeds, leases, plans, accounts and receipts, letters, marriage settlements, papers regarding the work of members of the family who were justices of the peace, and many others.

Flint tools have been found in Hanbury and it is believed it was an Iron Age hill fort.

The Norman church of St John the Baptist is built on a hill overlooking the village. Its extensions date mainly from the 1700s but a lot of the interior is still Norman. There was a large amount of repair work undertaken in 1860.

The woodland that stretches from Hanbury to the outskirts of Droitwich is known as Dodderhill Common, pronounced 'Doddrill' by the locals. Just outside Hanbury is Mere Hall, the largest surviving timber-framed building in Worcestershire. It was the home of the Bearcroft family from 1337 to 1976, a family whose ranks included many politicians, lawyers and soldiers.

Inkberrow

In modern times Inkberrow is well-known as the village on which Ambridge, the home of *The Archers*, is based. The church of St Peter is down a lane behind the Old Bull pub, supposedly the 'local' of Ambridge, and stands in a large churchyard. In Domesday Book the village is known as Interberga.

During the Civil War Charles I left his maps behind in Inkberrow as he journeyed to Worcester. These were later found and preserved for prosperity.

The Old Bull in Inkberrow has been immortalised on the radio. It was used as the example of a country pub for the series *The Archers* and is regularly visited by fans of the programme.

Kidderminster

Kidderminster is presumed to date back to Saxon times as the suffix 'minster' is a Saxon word, referring to a monastery or large church.

The parish church is St Mary's; a large church dating from the thirteenth century it has undergone a lot of repairs over the centuries and is now mainly fifteenth and sixteenth century design. Three other parishes were formed during the nineteenth century: St George's church was built in 1824, St John the Baptist in 1843, and St James' in 1872.

The carpet industry of Kidderminster goes back to the 1600s when the town was famous for its 'broadcloths', which were used as bed coverings and wall hangings. There is a reference from 1635 for a Kidderminster carpet on the inventory of a house in Essex. In the early 1700s there were 157 master weavers with 417 looms. But as fashions began to change, the industry went into decline and new ideas were sought.

It was John Pearsall in 1735 who came up with the idea of using the wall hangings as floor covering. In 1749 he went into partnership with John Broom and during travels across Europe was introduced to the system known as 'Brussels Weaving'. These carpets were made of mainly wool and were coarse and flat with a design on both sides making them reversible. They were cheaper than the hand-knotted carpets which had previously been made and were, therefore, accessible to a larger market. And with the opening of the Staffordshire–Worcester canal, Kidderminster carpets could now be exported abroad.

The carpets were originally woven as small pieces on small looms in the homes of the workers. But as carpets became larger the looms also had to become larger so the workers were unable to work in their own homes.

The first factory was Brinton's, which was built around 1820 by William Brinton. The family had been involved in the industry since the eighteenth century when, in 1783, William Brinton started enlisting workers in their own homes and gave them the wool to weave. He went on to run six looms in a small shed before his son, William, built the factory. A member of the sixth generation still manages the business today.

Another carpet manufacturer was Michael Tomkinson who purchased the British rights to the Axminster power loom in 1878.

William Charlton was the leader of the Great Strike of 1828. When he emigrated to America in 1845 his place as leader of the town's Chartist movement was taken by George Holloway. George had a colourful career as a carpet weaver, publican, auctioneer and liberal councillor.

In the 1850s power looms were introduced. At first, hand looms were able to compete as they enabled short runs of varying patterns. But factories not being suitable for conversion were soon unable to compete when all work could be carried out economically by the machines. Factories closed down and, with no employment available, weavers left Kidderminster for other parts of Britain.

In the 1890s there were protests against the poor working conditions of the weavers. These occasionally turned violent, but they were mainly peaceful and soldiers camped outside Kidderminster were not needed. However, the outcome was that Whittles took their factory to America and nearly half of Kidderminster with them.

There were about twenty carpet factories at the time of the First World War. The owners were also on the town council and they implemented a 'closed town' policy so no other industry could be allowed in. Those listed in an 1876 directory are:

John Adams
William Jesse Bannister
John Everard Banton
Henry Dixon, Jecks & Sons
H Fawcett & Co.
Greaves, Fidoe & Co.
W Green
Edward Perrin Griffin & Co.
Isaac Hampton
Edward Hughes & Sons
J Humphries & Sons
Clensmore Mills

Morton & Son
S B Palmer & Co.
F J Sellars & Co.
E Shaw & Co.
Tomkinson & Adams
Watson & Naylor
Moses Whittall & Co.
Willis H R Potter & Co.
Woodward Gower Wills & Co.
Grosvenor Woodward & Co.

Kings Norton, Northfield and Selly Oak

On 9 November 1911 the Birmingham Extension Act was passed and the boundaries of Birmingham with its neighbours were extended. As far as Worcestershire was concerned, this involved the parishes of Kings Norton and Northfield, including Selly Oak and Bourneville. They were now swallowed up into the city of Birmingham as its suburbs, and this does affect family history research.

The parish registers for Kings Norton are now in both Worcester Family History Centre and the Birmingham Archives in the Birmingham Library. The Bishops' Transcripts are in Worcester Family History Centre, and you will also find original material in both Worcester Record Office and the Birmingham Archives.

The parish registers for Northfield are only available in Birmingham Library, but the Bishops' Transcripts, and some original material, are in Worcester Family History Centre and Worcester Record Office. Selly Oak was created out of the parish of Northfield in 1862. Its registers and the majority of its original material are held at the Birmingham Archives. Bourneville did not become a parish until 1926 when it was created out of Selly Oak, so all its records are in the Birmingham Archives.

The parish church of Kings Norton is St Nicholas', which stands on the Green. It was built in the fifteenth century but it is believed a church existed there as far back as the twelfth century. Numerous repairs were undertaken in 1857 and several new windows were added in 1873. The church of St Lawrence dates from the twelfth century and is the parish church for Northfield. Two hundred acres of the Northfield parish were used to form the Selly Oak parish and St Mary's was built in 1861. St Francis of Assisi's was built in the 1920s to service the newly formed Bourneville parish.

Built on a hill above the flood plains of the River Rea, Kings Norton acquired its name by being on the edge of the royal hunting ground of Feckenham Forest and was known as the King's North Town. It still has a lot of country town character, with its village green and old buildings. The best-known building in Kings Norton is the Old Grammar School, a fifteenth-century building which stands next to the church in the graveyard.

A mayor of Worcester, John Noake, who visited Kings Norton in the 1850s, described the area around the green as a place 'where pigs and geese, and donkeys, and boys with their hoops, and little girls with babies nearly as heavy as themselves have rejoiced in rustic felicity from time immemorial.'

Kings Norton was a thriving agricultural village but during the Civil War on 17 October 1642 was also the centre of an encounter between Prince Rupert and Lord Willoughby of Parham. The prince and his men had been resting on the green when Willoughby made a surprise attack. On another occasion Queen Henrietta Maria passed through with replacement troops. She stayed at the Saracen's Head, while the army camped behind the church. The Saracen's Head is now the parish office and meeting room.

After the Enclosure Act of 1772 more agricultural labourers turned to industry and mills were built on the River Rea to use its power. Among these were the paper manufacturers of James Baldwin and the metal rolling mill of Wychall Mill. Gun barrels and bayonets were made at Hazelwell Mill, and a screw factory was built in 1862 by Nettlefolds.

Even in the early 1900s Northfield was a small rural community, but by the 1930s its farms and lands were quickly being redeveloped into housing estates. Northfield dates back to Saxon times but in Domesday Book it is owned by a Norman knight, William Fitz-Ansculf, and is known as Nordfield. In the 1800s it was also involved in nail making.

Selly Oak was part of the manor of Northfield. Its name is derived from 'selly', a terrace of land, and the oak tree which stood at the crossroads on the Bristol road. This oak tree was removed in 1909 for safety reasons, but part of its trunk was laid out in Selly Park.

A directory of 1876 referred to Selly Oak as being a manufacturing village containing nail and brick works. However the largest works in Selly Oak was Elliotts, a forger of 'sheathing for the bottoms and sides of vessels'. The factory had originally been a phosphorous factory owned by Sturges and built at the same time as the canal, but Elliotts had taken it over in 1853. With so much work available the population doubled. On the 1861 census there were 1,483 people in Selly Oak. In 1871 there were 2,854.

Bourneville was just an area of scattered farms and cottages until the Cadbury brothers arrived. John Cadbury and his sons had been manufacturing and selling chocolate from their shop in the centre of Birmingham for forty years. The sons, Richard and George Cadbury, had taken over the firm from their father in the 1870s and it was they who made the decision to move out to the country. They said that if the countryside was a good place in which to holiday then it could also be a good place in which to work; they also liked the idea of food being made in clean, healthy conditions. So the ideal spot for their 'Factory in the Garden' was found between the villages of Selly Oak and Kings Norton, some 4 miles south of Birmingham, and in September 1879 the first trainload of 230 employees arrived to start work in a totally new environment.

For fifteen years these workers travelled from Birmingham out into the country to work; then George Cadbury bought 120 acres of surrounding land and built the village of Bournville. 'Ville' for the French word of town (France being the place chocolate had first become popular) and 'Bourn', taken from the name of the stream which ran through the area. Here there were no monotonous streets around the factory, only tree-lined avenues and pleasant parkland, an area largely unchanged today.

Malvern

Malvern became well-known in the Victorian era as a place for 'taking the waters'. A directory of the 1870s says that despite being the home of thousands of invalids it had the lowest mortality rate in the country.

Two doctors, James Wilson and James Gully, set up a hydrotherapy practice in 1842 which was visited by many notable clients including Charles Dickens, Charles Darwin, Lord Tennyson and Florence Nightingale. At the clinic at Belle Vue their patients did not just drink the waters; they were also wrapped in damp cloths and encouraged to take dips in the cold spring water early in the morning. Long walks were also undertaken to drink from various fountains.

By the 1870s the 'taking of waters' was becoming less fashionable. Dr Wilson had died in 1867 and so in 1873 Dr Gully left Malvern. However Malvern water was still marketable. J Schweppe & Co. had been bottling Malvern water since 1851 and had supplied the Great Exhibition of 1851. This had told everyone of Malvern and its water and had established its reputation. Originally known as 'Malvern Soda' its name was changed in 1856 to 'Malvern Seltzer Water'. The first bottling well was Holy Well but a factory was built at Colwall in 1892 and water was piped from springs nearly a mile away. The factory today is owned by Coca-Cola and Schweppes Beverages Limited.

Malvern is also the base of the well-known manufacturers of the Morgan motor car. The Morgan Motor Company was established by Henry Frederick Stanley Morgan. Henry was born in 1881 the son of Henry George Morgan in Morton Jeffries, Herefordshire. His mother was the daughter of the vicar of St Matthias in Malvern Link, hence his connection to Malvern. On leaving school he worked as a draughtsman for the GWR works at Swindon, then in 1906, aged 25, he opened a garage in Malvern Link.

The three-wheeler was initially going to be a one-off, a bit of a folly for personal amusement, but as others showed interest Morgan decided to make a few more. He exhibited his prototype at the Olympia Motor Show in 1910, and in 1912 the Morgan Motor Company was formed. The directors were Henry Morgan senior and junior. The first factory was built in Worcester Road, Malvern, but a few years later in 1918 the present factory was opened on Pickersleigh Road.

The parish church of St Mary & St Michael was originally a Priory which was founded by Benedictine monks and built around 1085. It was restored in the reign of Henry VII and during the Dissolution of Monasteries his son, Henry VIII, allowed it to be saved by the parishioners who took it as their parish church. Other churches in the district are Christ Church at Barnard's Green, built in 1875; St Mary's, Guarlford, built in 1844, although it didn't become a parish until 1866; and Holy Trinity in North Malvern, founded in 1869.

Oddingley

Directories do not give Oddingley a very large entry. It is just described as a village and parish two miles south-east of Droitwich. But do you have a Richard Hemming in the family, who was a carpenter from Droitwich and who mysteriously disappeared in the early 1800s? Or perhaps you have an ancestor named Thomas Clewes who was the landlord of a public house in Dunhamstead? Then this story may interest you.

At around 5 o'clock in the evening of the 24th the peace of the small hamlet of Oddingley near Droitwich was shattered by the sound of a gunshot and a scream of 'murder'. Two people close to where the sound came from rushed to the scene. They found a man skulking in the hedge. When he saw them he dropped a bag he was carrying and ran. Inside the bag was a broken piece of a gun. At the same time they noticed a small fire; on further investigation they found it was the burning body of a man. He had been shot and his clothes set on fire by the wadding of the gun. This man was the vicar of Oddingley, the Reverend George Parker. The assailant was described as 'wearing a blue coat, and the fore part of his head rather bald'. It appeared that the gunshot had not killed the reverend outright, so the assailant had beat him about the head with the butt of the gun 'in so violent a manner that he broke it'.

Meanwhile, a carpenter from Droitwich by the name of Richard Hemming – who already had a reputation for being a violent man – had disappeared, never to be seen again. Twenty-four years later, in 1830, a barn was being built at nearby Netherwood Farm. Here the remains of a body were found. The farm was owned by Thomas Clewes, and at the inquest held at the Talbot Inn in Barbourne, Worcester, Clewes admitted knowing of the connection between the Reverend Parker's murder and the body.

The Reverend Parker was not a popular individual. He had been described as a hard and uncompromising man who was a stickler for rules, demanding the regulated one-tenth of everything a parishioner earned – even apparently down to their hedge cuttings. The villagers had banded together and, under the guidance of a farrier called James Taylor, Thomas Clewes and two other farmers called Banks and Barnett had hired Richard Hemming as a hit-man. In order not to be implicated the four men had enticed Hemming to the barn after the murder with the promise of food. Here, James Taylor had bludgeoned him to death and buried him.

By 1830 James Taylor was dead himself and the law was such that accomplices could not be charged without the 'principal' being charged, so Thomas Clewes and the other two were free to go. Thomas Clewes became landlord of a local pub, The Fir Tree at Dunhampstead, which became known as 'the murders' bar'. The walls were adorned with newspaper cuttings relating to the killing of the Reverend Parker.

Oldbury, according to an 1876 directory, stood in the middle of a district abounding in iron, coal and limestone; giving its inhabitants a wealth of employment. As well as the iron foundries and the edge tool works there were the alkali factories of Chance brothers and Co., the chemical works of Messrs Albright & Wilkes and Messrs Demuth & Co., and the steel works of Messrs Hunt.

Before the Industrial Revolution, Oldbury was a small hamlet in the parish of Halesowen and, prior to 1844, was in the county of Shropshire. As its industries grew, the population grew also and the town was swallowed up by the Black Country. Today, Oldbury is part of the Metropolitan Borough of Sandwell and its registers and archives are to be found in Sandwell Community History and Archives Service, in Smethwick Library.

Christ Church was described in 1876 as being a 'handsome brick building', which had been restored in 1867. It had been built in 1840 to replace a chapel which once stood there.

Pershore

The market town of Pershore, in olden times known as Persere, Pearsore or Periscoran, had its origins from its monastery. The land had been given to St Oswald, bishop of Worcester, by Ethelred of Mercia in AD 689. Oswald used it to build a monastery.

The Normans built an abbey here 400 years later. This was partly demolished during the Dissolution of Monasteries in 1540, but parishioners managed to salvage parts to restore as their parish church of Holy Cross. The town did suffer a decline after its monastery was gone and took a while to recover. The six-span medieval bridge which stretches across the River Avon was damaged in the Civil War, but restored soon afterwards.

The main industry here was wool-stapling. A wool-stapler would purchase wool from the sheep farmer then sort it into grades and sell it on to the merchants. It was in its heyday a very lucrative profession.

Pershore gained its name from the number of pear trees growing in the area, but it is now mainly known for its plums. George Crooks, then landlord of the Butcher's Arms in Church Street, found a seedling growing in Tiddesley Woods just outside Pershore and nurtured it. Now the Pershore Yellow Egg Plum is renowned in jam making circles.

For many years since, during the whole of August the Pershore Plum Festival takes over the town, accumulating with the grand finale on Bank Holiday Monday.

There are two parishes within Pershore – St Andrew's and Holy Cross – and its hamlets include Walcot, Pensham, Wadborough and Broughton.

Powick

Known as Poiwic in medieval times and Powyke in later times, Powick is largely known for its mental hospital 'The County and City of Worcester Lunatic Asylum'. Built in 1847 it could hold 200 patients, rising to 365 after an extension was built in 1858. However, an 1876 directory states that in 1875 it held 319 male patients and 392 female patients. It contained workshops for various trades and had a farm and brew house. In 1879 it even formed its own band with Edward Elgar as its musical director. The staff thought that music would be a relaxing treatment for the patients, so those members of staff who could play a musical instrument got together. The asylum was also famous for using LSD as a treatment for severe mental illnesses. It closed in 1989 and has been developed into a housing estate.

Powick is also known as the place where the first skirmish of the Civil War took place in 1642 and where the last one took place in 1651. Holes made in Powick Church by musket balls are still visible.

Redditch

At any given time someone, in some part of the world, is using a needle made in Redditch. Although originally only a part-time occupation undertaken by the wives and children of farmers and tradespeople, needle-making became a growing trade in eighteenth-century Redditch.

In 1702 William Sheward had set up a business buying packets of needles from individual makers and selling them to the general public. In return he obtained supplies of wire for these needle makers. This lay the foundations for the industry to develop.

In 1730 Henry Millward & Sons was founded by Symon Millward; it was to become the longest-established firm in Redditch (as stated in *The*

Forge Mill Museum, once a working mill, now tells the full story of the needle-making history of the region, as well as showing the different processes involved in the making of the needles.

Victoria County History of Worcestershire, 1906). Seeing his success, other wealthy businessmen began setting up in the area. But although factories were springing up over the town, the cottage industry did not fold. A lot of the work was still undertaken by women and children in their homes. For example a needle-straightener would have her own small anvil and spend all day tapping at the needles with a small hammer to straighten them. As her daughters grew up, they too would help.

Needle makers' cottages were recognisable by the windows, which were wide in proportion to their height. This provided plenty of light for the fiddly work. In 1824 it was estimated that a needle-maker and his family could produce 500 needles a week.

Around this time Peter Shrimpton came to Redditch from Long Crendon, followed by other members of his family, and set up their works here. They were joined by a steady influx of other workers from Long

Crendon and so by 1850 it was estimated that 200,000 needles a week were being made in Redditch and exported all over the world.

The needle-making process went through many procedures. A needle started as a strip of wire cut into the size of two needles. A pointer sharpened both ends on a grindstone. This was the highest paid job in the needle industry due to the high mortality rate; pointers were prone to breathe in the dust of wire particles which sprayed from the grindstone, causing lung diseases, known as 'pointers' rot'.

Two eyes were then made in the centre of the wire by the stampers, and then it was then sent to the spitter, who split the needles into two by feeding them through a handheld spit and cutting them through the centre. This work was also undertaken by women in their own homes. The separated needles were now sent to the furnace for hardening. This process usually damaged the shape of the needle so they were then sent to the needle-straightener. The needles were then sent to the scouring mill to be polished.

During the migration of workers from Long Crendon the needle maker Kirby Beard relocated in 1848 to try to keep a certain amount of workers there. However, with no railway built in Long Crendon when one was being built in Redditch, the firm and its workers moved back to Redditch in 1862.

Needles were not the only industry which put Redditch on the map. Polycarp Allcock started his small fishing tackle business in 1803 which his son, Samuel, eventually took over and expanded. By 1880 it was claimed that Samuel Allcock & Co. was the largest and oldest manufacturer of fish hooks in the world. In the 1960s the company amalgamated with others under the control of an American, Henry Shakespeare, and in the 1980s the turnover was in excess of £4 million. Again, part of this industry could be done at home, in particular fly dressing, which was done by women.

Many firms manufactured both needles and fishing tackle; others specialised in one or the other. A list from an 1876 directory shows the number of mills and businesses associated with the two trades:

–Samuel Allcock
–James Avery

–R Bartleet & Sons

–William Bartleet & Sons

–Arthur George Baylis & Sons

–Thomas Baylis & Co.

–G W Beard & Co.

–Alfred Booker & Co.

–William Boulton & Sons – 'sole manufacturers of the Queen's 'Ne Plus
    Ultra' triple prize needles.'

–William Clarke & Sons

–James Dyson & Co.

–John English & Sons

–Fletcher, Westwood & Co.

–Harrison & Bartleet

–Richard Hemming & Son

–Hoseph Holyoake & Son

–John James & Sons

–Kirby Beard & Sons

–Henry Millward & Sons

–Joseph Mogg & Co.

–Alfred Shrimpton & Son

–S Thomas & Sons

–Richard Turner & Co.

–Joseph Warrin & Son

–William Woodfield & Sons

There were two other industries for which Redditch became famous:
Herbert Terry & Sons was founded in 1855 in a small workshop. At first
the company produced clips and metal fittings for use on crinolines, but
went on to specialise in springs to coincide with the growth of the motor
industry in the area, then, in the twentieth century, to produce specialities
such as exercise equipment and anglepoise lamps.

The Royal Enfield Cycle Company and its famous Enfield motorbikes
grew up from a small cycle company called George Townsend & Co. It
became the Enfield Cycle Company in 1897 and in 1899 expanded into the

Close to Forge Mill Museum are the foundations of St Stephen's Chapel. St Stephen's was in use in the seventeenth and eighteenth centuries. It was built with stones salvaged from the destruction of Bordesley Abbey during the Dissolution. In the early nineteenth century it was moved stone by stone up the hill to be rebuilt on what was to become known as Church Green. The foundations of the chapel are still visible and a number of gravestones are still standing. However, those that are still legible give only an initial and year.

motor industry, which resulted in the production of the famous motorbike in 1912. The factory closed in 1967 but the industrial units that its building was turned into still bear the name – Enfield Industrial Estate, with the words Royal Enfield still visible on the roofs.

St Stephen's stands on the top of the hill which Redditch grew up around. Originally Redditch belonged to the Tardebigge parish, but a small chapel had been left behind when Bordesley Abbey was destroyed. In 1805 this chapel was becoming too small to accommodate the fast-growing community and was taken down stone by stone. These stones were then transported up the hill and rebuilt, becoming known as the 'Chapel on the Green'. In 1855 this was replaced by a larger church and Redditch, having become a busy industrial town, became a parish of its own.

Stourbridge and Old Swinford

Sturesbridge appears on a 1255 Worcestershire assize roll. Named after an ancient bridge over the River Stour it was a medieval town which belonged to the manor of Swynford and included the hamlets of Lye, Lye Waste and Wollaston. As the area expanded in the 1850s and '60s the Old Swinford Parish divided to form new parishes, and Stourbridge built its own churches. St Mary's, Old Swinford, was the original church; St John's, on the eastern side of Stourbridge, was built in 1862; but St Thomas' in Market Street, built in 1866, became the parish church of Stourbridge. Christchurch in Lye was also built in 1866.

It was in this district the Foley family made their fortune, powering their forges and mills from water wheels on the river. Richard Foley (1580–1657) was the son of a nailer from Dudley. He became a partner in an ironworks in South Staffordshire but, while visiting Sweden, he discovered a new design in slitting mills (a type of watermill which slits bars of iron into rods). With this procedure he made his fortune and his descendants not only followed him into the iron industry but also became members of Parliament. His son Robert became high sheriff of Worcestershire in 1671 and another son, Thomas, amassed a large enough fortune to build Witley Court, where the Foleys lived until the house was was sold to Earl Dudley in 1837.

Thomas Foley was also responsible for the building of a charity school for boys. Known as the Old Swinford Hospital it gave boys from poorer families the chance of a better education; it still stands today but is now a private boarding school.

All Foley's sons became involved in politics: Thomas became the member of Parliament for Worcestershire in the latter half of the seventeenth century; Paul became speaker of the House of Commons in 1695 after a colourful career which saw him imprisoned during the Monmouth Rebellion; Philip was the member of Parliament for Bewdley. His grandsons Edward and Richard became members of Parliament for Droitwich, and their brother Thomas was created Baron Foley in 1712. The family was Presbyterian and helped establish a church in the area.

In early times Stourbridge was surrounded by hills and the heathland was an area suitable for sheep grazing. With clean water readily available to wash the wool, Stourbridge flourished as a prosperous woollen centre. But with the opening of the Stourbridge Canal in 1779 there followed a rapid expansion of the ironworks. Others were also becoming prosperous – John Bradley and Co. and Foster, Rastrick & Co. The first steam locomotive to run on a commercial line in America was built in Stourbridge and was known as the Stourbridge Lion.

There are two conflicting stories of how glass first came to be made in Stourbridge. Both legends concern the same family and the same era in the mid-sixteenth century. One concerns Huguenot refugees from Lorraine and Hungary named Hanezah. They were musicians and first went to London but, not being accepted in society there, they travelled north to the Midlands. Making their camp at Lye Waste they discovered the fire clay there was similar to the clay they had used at home for making glass. They called their new home Hungary Hill – as it is still known today. Another story has it that a John Carre, who was given a licence to manufacture glass in the area, asked Henzoil Henzey to bring his skills to this country. Henzey was later joined by other glass manufacturers – the Tyzackes. Whichever story is correct there is evidence of three glasshouses being owned by a Joshua Henzey in 1615.

In the late eighteenth century the principal owners of glasshouses were Lord Foley, Edward Hickman and Mr Millward. In 1906 the glass manufacturers were The Stourbridge Glass and Gripalite Tile Company Ltd and Messrs Thomas Webb & Son of the Stourbridge Glass Works. Thomas Webb's were the most famous of glass manufacturers and had been established since 1829. They remained in business until 1990, although the family name of Webb was no longer involved, when they were taken over by Edinburgh Crystal.

Other firms advertising in an 1876 directory are:

–J. Aston Wood & Co., makers of chain, cables, anchors, spade and shovels, scythes, hammers, nails and frying pans among other things.
–John Evason & Co., makers of anvils, spades and chains.
–Charles Ward, makers of iron gates and fencing.

Stourport

Stourport was just a small hamlet with a handful of cottages when James Brindley built the canal adjoining the Severn and the Trent in 1766. For the following 200 years it was a busy inland port, with numerous warehouses springing up around the five basins at the junctions of the two waterways. It was known as one of the busiest inland ports in England and even in the early 1700s pleasure boats could be found here.

Originally Stourport had been known as Lower Mitton, but as the hamlet developed into a town it took its new name from a neighbouring inn. Family historians should note that even for the years it was known as Lower Mitton, the registers will be found indexed under Stourport.

Stourport still gives the appearance of a typical Georgian town and the four basins now left are always filled with numerous holiday boats of all shapes and sizes.

Tardebigge

The name is derived from the Saxon church built on the hill in AD 974 and means 'tower on the hill'. A Norman church was built in the eleventh century but the tower collapsed in 1775. Work on the present church, St Bartholomew's, began in 1777. However, services still took place during the rebuilding of the church as the parish registers show baptisms, marriages and burials entered for those years.

Agriculture was, and still is to a certain degree, the chief industry in the area. But since the building of the Worcester to Birmingham Canal, Tardebigge has become famous for its thirty locks which climb the hillside, one after the other; known collectively as the Tardebigge Flight.

Nearby Hewell Grange was once the home of the Windsor family, the earls of Plymouth. The present house was built in 1885–1892 and is now a prison. The estate was originally the property of Bordesley Abbey in Redditch and was acquired by Henry VIII after the Dissolution of the Monasteries. Andrew, Lord Windsor, owned an estate near Windsor at Stanwell, so was persuaded by Henry to exchange his lands for those of Bordesley Abbey. The Windsors eventually became an influential family in the area; many streets and roads are named after them. The earldom of Plymouth was bestowed on them in 1682, after Thomas Windsor Hickman distinguished himself in the Battle of Naseby in 1645.

On the 1901 census at Springhill, Webheath Lane, Tardebigge are Samuel and Hannah Middleton aged 47 and 50 respectively. Living next door is Harriet Hassell, a widow aged 74. Are they in your family tree? A year later their story had made the headlines in the local newspaper.

On the night of 10 May 1902 Mrs Hassell was woken by the Middletons, who were arguing. This was not unusual; Hannah had spent most of her married life putting up with Samuel's drinking so Harriet just turned over and went back to sleep. Two hours later she woke up again and this time she could smell smoke. Both cottages were on fire.

Samuel had murdered his wife, covered her body with bacon fat and straw and set fire to it. He was found the following night 12 miles away on a lane between Himbleton and Crowle. When charged he said that Hannah had been nagging him so much he had tried to leave, but when she had tried to stop him he had hit her with a poker. His was the first execution under the new law whereby there was no black flag to signal when the execution was taking place, which it was felt 'often aroused interest in minds of morbidly inclined people to assemble outside the prison'. Also the chaplain, instead of reciting the service for the burial while the man was still alive, now waited until the executioner had done his job and the prisoner was dead.

Tenbury

'The Town in the Orchard' was the term used to describe Tenbury. It became a spa town in 1840 after the first spring was found in 1839, and contains many elaborate Victorian buildings. The college of St Michael was built in 1856 and prepared the sons of young gentlemen for inclusion in the higher forms of larger public schools. Its speciality was in the music and choral classes.

Temebury, as it was known, was an ancient town on an important river crossing. In 1615 it lay on the main road between Wales and London. It contained and was surrounded by many orchards and hop yards but these are much diminished today. Every September the Wyre Forest Railway would arrive in the Teme Valley bringing hundreds from the Black Country to pick hops. For them it was a working holiday.

The church of St Mary the Virgin was rebuilt in the nineteenth century after flood damage and only the tower remains of the old building.

Worcester

Standing majestically over the River Severn is Worcester Cathedral. It was founded in AD 680 but rebuilt in 1084 by Wulfston, bishop of Worcester. Born c.1008 he became a monk at Worcester Cathedral and rose through the ranks. He was confessor to King Harold but after 1066 was allowed to remain bishop, therefore maintaining Anglo-Saxon values together with the new ideas of the Normans. The cathedral was badly damaged in the Civil War and underwent redevelopment after the Restoration, but it was not until 1864–75 that the major repair works took place.

King John was buried here in 1216. He enjoyed hunting in the area and had visited the shrine of St Wulfstan in the cathedral.

Porcelain was originally only made in the Far East, but Dr John Wall and William Davies experimented with the manufacturing of different types of porcelain. They enlisted the financial help of a group of local businessmen and in 1751 their blue coloured porcelain was introduced. In 1757 the use of transfer printing was developed and many new designs were soon being produced. John Wall spent twenty-five years building the business and when he retired William Davies took sole charge. When he died it was bought by a London agent, Thomas Flight, for his sons John and Joseph.

When the Flight brothers took over the factory they developed other techniques and on the advice of King George III, who had visited the

Worcester factory, a shop was opened in London close to Piccadilly Circus. Robert Chamberlain had been head of the decorating department for John Wall. He had left to open his own premises, first in King Street then Severn Street, with a shop on the High Street. He returned and joined the Flight brothers and now many new ideas and products were produced.

Trade began to wane in 1833, mainly due to the cheaper competition such as Staffordshire stone china. But the Great Exhibition of 1851 put an end to that and interest in porcelain was renewed. This renewed interest also opened a path for the making of porcelain figurines, and by the late nineteenth century Worcester was recognised as one of the leading manufacturers of all porcelain. In 1852 the company was acquired by W.H. Kerr and R.W. Binns. It became the Worcester Royal Porcelain Co. Ltd in 1862, although the works had had a royal warrant since 1788 following a visit by George III.

Another ex-worker who had left the company in 1801 to set up on his own was Thomas Grainger. His factory stayed productive for 100 years through three generations: Thomas, his sons George and Henry, and his grandson, Frank. The Grainger factory was acquired by the Royal Worcester Company in 1902 when Frank emigrated to Canada.

The glove trade in Worcester dates back to 1496 when a Glovers' Guild was set up in Worcester. However it is believed the trade had already been in existence long before that. In 1642 only leather gloves were made as it was against the law to make gloves of linen or cloth. A fine of 6s 8d was levied.

The glove-making centre lay between present day Deansway and the waterfront in St Andrew's parish. The spire of St Andrew's church became known as 'The Glover's Needle'. With a height of 155ft, rising from a 20ft diameter base – itself rising from a tower of 90ft high – it is easy to see how it got its name. The old buildings here and along the Dolday and Newport Street became the core; however they also became the urban slum areas of the city.

Thomas Price (c.1814) and father of the Victorian novelist Mrs Henry Wood (who wrote the novel East Lynne) was a glove manufacturer here and her book 'Mrs Haliburton's Troubles' is based on the glovers of Worcester. Up to the 1840s gloves were made in small workshops run by a master with

St Andrew's dates back to the twelfth century; the tower was built in the fifteenth century and the spire rebuilt in 1751. The church fell into disuse and the main building was demolished in the 1940s because it was so dilapidated. Only the tower and spire remain. A garden was established where the churchyard once was and opened in commemoration of the coronation.

three or four journeymen or apprentices cutting gloves. The pieces were then sewed together by home workers in cottages around Worcestershire. Gloves were hawked around by the master at fairs, at markets or by visiting regular customers.

The glove making industry was entering its heyday in the late 1700s when 5,000 people were employed in the glove trade, either in the city or surrounding villages. This trend continued into the 1800s and at its peak the Worcester glove industry included 150 manufacturers who employed over 30,000 people. However, the slump came in 1826 when the government lifted import taxes on foreign goods and suddenly the price of French gloves fell in line with those made in Worcester. There was now mass unemployment in the city. Many glovers became boot and shoe makers to take advantage of their leather-working skills. By 1884 only twelve were left. These were:

Robert Bach – Park Street
Thomas Bach – Lowesmoor
William T. Burlington – Sidbury
Dent Allcroft & Co. – Palace Yard
Firkins & Co. – Foregate Street
Abel Foulkes – Bridge Street
Fownes Bros & Co. – Talbot Street
Thomas Henry Golding – Castle Place
Richard Guise – St Nicholas Street
Joseph Potter – Newport Street
Charles Henry Redgrave – New Street
Thomas Henry Smith – High Street

Only two firms did eventually survive – Dents Allcroft & Co. and Fownes Bros & Co.

John Dent had started his company in 1777 in the way previously described. He worked in the workshop while William Dent travelled around the fairs and markets, eventually acquiring regular customers. By 1833 Dent was employing 133 workers (although some of these were employed in the

London factory). The Dents were considered the top-class craftsmen in the manufacture of fine leather gloves and amassed a fortune.

In 1837 John & William Dent acquired Sudeley Castle in Gloucestershire and began a restoration programme on a castle which had been left derelict for 200 years. Restoration was finally completed by their nephew John Croucher Dent when he inherited the property in 1855.

Fownes factory on City Walls Road is now a hotel. The original factory had been built in 1882 after the firm had first established themselves in London. Following their move to Worcester, Fownes Glove Company employed more than 1,000 employees and was one of the world's leading glove makers. They eventually became an international company with factories and offices in many parts of the world. But as fashions changed, the glove industry went into decline, and the Worcester factory closed in 1974. All the business was transferred to Warminster in Wiltshire and the building in Worcester lay derelict until 1985 when it was rescued and became the Fownes Hotel.

The Vulcan Ironworks, situated on Cromwell Street, on the west side of the canal, were originally set up by Thomas Clunes in 1857. A directory at the time lists him as an iron and brass founder, but the company was to become a worldwide manufacturer of railway signals. Clunes was joined by McKenzie and Holland in 1861 who were former employees of the Oxford, Worcester and Wolverhampton Railway Company. Walter Holland became a JP and was mayor of Worcester from 1878 to 1881, and again in 1887. The company merged with other signal manufacturers in 1901.

Hardy and Padmore, the Worcester Foundry, was formed in 1814 when Robert and John Hardy arrived in Worcester from Scotland. In 1829 Richard Padmore moved from Shropshire and joined the company and the business went from strength to strength until the 1940s. Its success then began to decline and the works closed in 1967. Over those years the company produced many castings which are still visible today, such as the 'Dolphin' lamps of the Westminster Embankment and the railway bridge across Foregate Street in Worcester.

The tile houses of Worcester were mainly found in the north-eastern part of the town around Lowesmoor. The industry seems to have been in existence since the fifteenth century. In more modern times tiles were made by James Hancock & son and James Hadley & Sons, who were established in 1896. There was also Webb's Worcester Tileries, who were established in 1873 by Mr H.C. Webb of Astwood Road, Worcester.

Other industries found a home in Worcester. Messrs J.L. Larkworthy & Co. of Lowesmoor made agricultural tools and brushes. Brooms were made by Smith & Co. of High Street, who was established in 1797, and also by Pemberton & Son of Broad Street. Another well-know name associated with Worcester is Lea & Perrins the 'original and genuine Worcestershire sauce' manufacturer. They were established around 1843 in Bank Street and Broad Street, and then in 1897 in Midland Street. Vinegar was also made in Worcester by Hill, Evans & Co Ltd. The company was formed by William Hill and Edward Evans in 1830.

For the wealthy city merchants of Worcester, home was in the northern suburb of Claines. A large and extensive parish, it is unique in that it has a public house built within the grounds of the parish church of St John the Baptist. The Mug House is believed to be about 600 years old. Given that it is surrounded by the graves of hundreds of past residents, it is not surprising that it purports to be haunted.

Directory of Family History Centres, Libraries and Other Useful Sources

Worcester Record Office
County Hall, Spetchley, Worcester, WR5 2NP
01905 765312

Worcester Family History Centre
Trinity Street, Worcester, WR1 2PW
01905 765922

Dudley Record Office
Mount Pleasant Street, Coseley, West Midlands
01384 812770

Sandwell Community History and Archives Service
Smethwick Library, High Street, Smethwick
0121 558 0497

Birmingham Archives & Heritage
Central Library, Chamberlain Square, Birmingham
0121 303 4217/4549/4220

Alvechurch Library
Tanyard Lane, Alvechurch
0121 445 3049

Bewdley Library
Load Street, Bewdley
01299 403303

Broadway Library
Leamington Road, Broadway
01386 858747

Bromsgrove Library
Stratford Road, Bromsgrove
01527 575855

Droitwich Library
Victoria Square, Droitwich
01905 773292

Evesham Library
Oat Street, Evesham
01386 442291

Kidderminster Library
Market Street, Kidderminster
01562 824500

Kings Norton Library
Pershore Road South, Kings Norton
0121 464 1532

Malvern Library
Graham Road, Malvern
01684 561223

Pershore Library
Church Street, Pershore
01386 553320

Redditch Library
15 Market Place, Redditch
01527 63291

Stourport on Severn Library
County Buildings, Worcester Street, Stourport
01299 822866

Tenbury Wells Library
24 Teme Street, Tenbury Wells
01584 810285

Upton upon Severn Library
School Lane, Upton on Severn
01684 592176

Worcester City Library
Foregate Street, Worcester
01905 765312

The Newspaper Library
Colindale Avenue, London, NW9 5HE
020 741 27353

Certificates

General Register Office
Smedley Hydro, Trafalgar Road, Southport, Merseyside, PR8 2JD
www.gro.gov.uk/gro

Wills

Postal Searches Department
1st Floor, Castle Chambers, 5 Clifford Street, York, YO1 9RG

Websites

General Family History Sites

www.ancestry.co.uk
www.findmypast.com
www.familysearch.org
www.a2a.org.uk

Military Sites

www.cwgc.org
www.military-genealogy.com
www.roll-of-honour.com

Museums

Worcester City Museum and Art Gallery
Foregate Street, Worcester
01905 25371

The Worcester Porcelain Museum
Severn Street, Worcester
01905 21247

Worcestershire County Museum
Hartlebury Castle, Hartlebury
01299 250416

Forge Mill Museum
Needle Mill Lane, Riverside, Redditch
01527 62509

Avoncroft Museum
Redditch Road, Bromsgrove
01527 831363

Malvern Museum
Priory Gatehouse, Abbey Road, Malvern
01684 567811

Bewdley Museum
Load Street, Bewdley
01299 403573

Black Country Living Museum
Tipton Road, Dudley
0121 557 9643

Kidderminster Carpet Museum and Archives
Unit 27/28, MCF Complex, 60 New Road, Kidderminster
01562 69001 (by arrangement only)

New Library and History Centre

In 2012 a new building will be opened. The present Worcester Record
Office at County Hall and Worcester Family History Centre in Trinity
Street will be housed together in a new building next to the University
campus. The building will also include the Worcester Library. Construction
on the site began on 1 February 2010 at The Butts, Worcester. Regular
updates will appear on the Worcester Record Office web page.

Family History Societies

BMSGHS
Worcester branch
www.worcesterbmsghs.co.uk

Your Family History Notes

Visit our website and discover thousands of other History Press books.

www.thehistorypress.co.uk